The Next Frontier in SME Ratings

Saveshen Pillay

The Next Frontier in SME Ratings

Improving Access to Credit and Business Opportunities for the World's Largest Business Segment

palgrave
macmillan

Saveshen Pillay
Credit Rating Analytics
Sandton, South Africa

ISBN 978-3-031-54014-1 ISBN 978-3-031-54015-8 (eBook)
https://doi.org/10.1007/978-3-031-54015-8

Cover illustration: MIHAI ANDRITOIU/Alamy Stock Photo

This Palgrave Macmillan imprint is published by the registered company Springer Nature Switzerland AG
The registered company address is: Gewerbestrasse 11, 6330 Cham, Switzerland

Paper in this product is recyclable.

Preface

Small- and medium-sized enterprises (SMEs) have been plagued with the perennial issue of access to funding. Whilst there have been concerted efforts to ameliorate this ubiquitous issue, these efforts have had a tenuous effect when we examine the significant credit gap that exists in both developed and developing markets. The SME credit rating concept has proven to be effective at improving access to finance and proliferating business opportunities. However, the problem is that the concept is not widely available, and there is limited knowledge of its potential benefits; this book has been written to address this by increasing awareness of the concept. I introduce the public sector model, which has been quite effective at providing these services on a broad-scale basis. There has been much talk of a public sector credit rating model, but there is almost no awareness about the public sector SME credit rating model outside of Europe. My firm, Credit Rating Analytics, is currently assisting a sovereign state in creating the first public sector grading agency in emerging markets, which will be the world's largest upon completion (public or private). I include some of the insights gained from that project and provide a stepwise breakdown of how other countries can create similar public sector grading/rating agencies. The COVID-19 pandemic has devastated the ability of SMEs to access credit facilities, and I believe there needs to be an out-of-the-box solution to rectify the funding challenges that SMEs encounter. In my opinion, the SME credit rating concept could be one of these out-of-the-box solutions which could revolutionise the SME sector and propel overall economic growth. The book quotes the benefits of these ratings, the concept's development in different regions, and is one of the first to unpack how it can be brought to fruition by countries that are keen on its adoption.

Sandton, South Africa

Mr. Saveshen Pillay
www.creditratinganalytics.co.za

Acknowledgements

I would like to extend my profound gratitude to all of the stakeholders I have had the privilege of collaborating with on this groundbreaking concept. These stakeholders encompass a wide array of organisations and individuals, including credit rating agencies from around the globe that have been instrumental in shaping the SME credit rating industry. Their expertise, innovation, and dedication have provided invaluable insights and laid a strong foundation for the work presented in this book. Special acknowledgement goes to the team at the World Bank Group. Their trust in my firm, Credit Rating Analytics, to undertake an important project on the concept of SME credit ratings has been a significant milestone in my professional journey. The insights garnered from this project have served as a profound source of inspiration, motivating me to write this book. Many of the key findings from this collaboration are quoted in the sections below, providing a rich tapestry of knowledge and practical guidance. Additionally, I am deeply grateful to the donors that we are currently working with, whose generous funding has enabled Credit Rating Analytics to partner with a sovereign state in creating the first public sector SME grading agency in emerging markets. This landmark project represents a monumental step forward in the development of SME credit ratings, and the critical insights gained from this initiative are shared within this publication. These insights are intended to serve as a valuable resource for other governments aspiring to establish similar organisations and enhance their financial ecosystems. Furthermore, I would like to acknowledge the myriad contributions of numerous other individuals and organisations who have supported this endeavour. Their collective efforts have enriched this book, making it a comprehensive and practical guide for advancing SME credit ratings.

On a deeply personal note, I wish to extend my heartfelt gratitude to my wife, whose unwavering support and encouragement have been instrumental in the completion of this book. From the very inception of Credit Rating Analytics, she has been my rock, offering steadfast motivation and insightful advice at every turn. Her belief in my vision has been a constant source of inspiration, driving me to overcome the many challenges that come with writing a book whilst managing a demanding consulting firm. Her sacrifices, whether in terms of personal time or shared responsibilities, have been innumerable, and her unwavering motivation has kept me focused and driven. To my parents, words cannot express the depth of my gratitude. Your relentless hard work and dedication over the years have shaped the person I am today. The values of perseverance, integrity, and commitment that you instilled in me have been the cornerstone of my professional and personal life. Your guidance has not only enabled me to embark on this ambitious journey but has also provided the moral and ethical framework that underpins this publication. The lessons you imparted, often through your own actions and sacrifices, have taught me the importance of resilience and the power of a strong work ethic. For this, I am eternally grateful, and I am keenly aware that there is no way to adequately repay the immense debt I owe you. To my grandparents, this book is as much a testament to your legacy as it is a product of my efforts. Your extraordinary journey, marked by resilience and a relentless pursuit of self-education under challenging circumstances, has paved the way for our future generations. The hardships you endured and the determination you demonstrated have been a profound source of inspiration. Your story is a reminder of the strength and fortitude that runs through our family, and it is your legacy of hard work and perseverance that has enabled me to achieve my dreams. This book is dedicated to you in recognition of the path you forged and the foundations you laid for our success. Lastly, to my extended family and friends, thank you for your constant support and encouragement. Your belief in me, even during the most trying times, has been invaluable. Each one of you has played a role in this journey, and I am grateful for your presence and contributions. This book is not just my achievement; it is a collective accomplishment made possible by the love, support, and encouragement of those around me.

About This Book

This book offers comprehensive insights into the SME credit rating concept and explores its broader applicability in both developing and developed economies. It delves into the general principles and highlights both private and public sector models. Drawing from the author's firm's ongoing engagement with an emerging market nation to establish an SME grading system, this publication integrates some of the valuable insights derived from that project. The book is systematically divided into four main parts, each structured to provide a nuanced understanding and contextualisation of the SME credit rating concept. The latter chapters emphasise the implementation of this concept in countries aiming to enhance the availability of such ratings. An overview of the four main parts is as follows:

Part I provides an overview of the existing SME industry and unpacks its prospects in a post-COVID-19 environment. The SME industry has come under tremendous pressure over the past few years, and we examine its historical and projected performance over the period ahead. The part also focuses on SME-related themes linked to the SME credit rating concept, such as access to finance and access to market. We examine these concepts to create a sound foundation for the book, which will assist in contextualising how the SME credit rating concept can ameliorate some of the issues that are plaguing this important sector.

Part II introduces the SME credit rating concept and outlines its development over the last two decades. It will provide a sequential breakdown of the industry's growth across various regions, and we will delve into the many factors that have impeded its development. We also unpack some of the benefits of these ratings, which have been outlined in previous empirical studies and will showcase the potential benefits of these ratings to alternative lending channels. A large number of these alternative lending channels currently operate without these ratings; however, stakeholder outcomes could be significantly optimised if the SME rating concept complemented these existing lending mechanisms.

Part III unpacks the public sector credit rating model and how it can be utilised within the SME credit rating industry. We explore how the public sector model has worked in countries that have embraced the concept and provide recommendations on how it could be introduced into other countries. It should be noted that the public sector credit rating model has garnered a great deal of attention in the aftermath of the global financial crisis, with many practitioners and stakeholders calling for its adoption as an alternative to the private sector credit rating industry. Whilst the majority of these attempts have not amounted to much, the public sector SME credit rating model has flourished in Europe and has had a positive impact on access to finance within this crucial sector. The concluding chapters of this part outline how the public sector SME credit rating model can be brought to fruition. The author's consulting firm (Credit Rating Analytics) is currently working as a lead advisor to an emerging market country to create the world's largest SME grading agency (public or private). The grading agency in question focuses on both access to market and credit, and some of the insights gained from that project are outlined in this part.

Part IV—This part includes recommendations on how to create a private sector SME credit rating industry. One should be mindful that having a private or public sector industry is not mutually exclusive as both can complement each other and operate concurrently, as is the case in Europe. The focus should not be on choosing between the two options but rather on evaluating the feasibility of establishing both, each catering to different market segments. Within this part, we showcase what is required to create a private sector SME credit rating industry and subsequently introduce the private sector SME credit rating ecosystem model. The ecosystem model is a collective approach by various stakeholders who are all working together to achieve the common goal of access to finance. We unravel how this innovative concept can be put into practice and showcase how it has worked in other countries.

A brief breakdown of some of the important chapters within the four parts is as follows:

Chapter Two—An overview of the existing SME industry. This includes an overview of the current SME industry and the impact of external events on access to credit.
Chapter Three—An introduction to the SME credit rating concept. This chapter introduces the SME credit rating concept, provides a mapping of the existing industry, and highlights the technical dynamics behind these ratings.
Chapter Four—The benefits of the SME credit rating industry. Here, we explore how these ratings can benefit individual countries where they are made available. We examine some of the empirical studies that have been conducted that measured the impact these ratings have had on rated entities. The chapter will also cover some of the broader benefits of these ratings on traditional and non-traditional funding channels.
Chapter Five—An introduction to the public sector credit rating model. This chapter introduces the public sector credit rating model and unpacks why it can be a viable solution for governments in a post-COVID-19 environment.
Chapter Six—Practical applications of the public sector SME credit rating model. The public sector SME credit rating model is an often unknown concept in most jurisdictions but is utilised by central banks in Europe. We provide insights into how these organisations are operationally set up and effectively provide these services.
Chapter Seven—Bringing the public sector SME credit rating concept into fruition. Here, we examine expert insights into how this innovative concept can be brought to fruition. I will provide a broad overview of how the organisation could be structured to ensure that it is impactful and achieves its intended objectives.
Chapter Eight—Recommendations for the creation of an SME credit rating industry. Herein is an outline of how to create a robust SME credit rating industry and provides examples of countries that have managed to do so successfully.
Chapter Nine—An introduction to the SME credit rating ecosystem approach. The final chapter introduces the concept of "SME credit rating ecosystems". This is essentially a coordinated effort to enhance access to finance for SMEs by promoting the use of SME credit ratings. The ecosystem consists of SME credit rating agencies, ministries linked to the SME sector, the central bank, stock exchanges, and commercial lenders.

Contents

About the Author

Saveshen Pillay is the chief executive officer at Credit Rating Analytics, a specialist advisory firm focusing on the credit rating industry. He holds a Master's Degree in International Banking & Finance *(Cum Laude),* a Postgraduate Diploma in Finance, Banking & Investment Management, a B.Com. Degree in Economics, and has completed level 2 of the CFA program. Moreover, Saveshen has led numerous high-level projects and has presented at major events such as the African Union's 4th Specialized Technical Committee on Finance, Monetary Affairs, Economic Planning, and Integration (one of the largest economic events on the African continent). As mentioned, his company is assisting a sovereign state in creating the first public sector SME grading agency in emerging markets, which will also be the world's largest SME grading agency upon completion (public or private). Credit Rating Analytics has completed some interesting projects within the credit rating space which include, but not limited to: (1) They assisted the African Union and the United Nations Economic Commission For Africa with a feasibility study which looked into the prospects of setting up a public sector credit rating agency, (2) The company served as one of the lead advisors to the World Bank Group on the concept of SME credit ratings and provided three innovative solutions on how the concept can be scaled up globally, (3) Funded by the OSF and in collaboration with the Credit Rating Research Initiative and leading academic institutions in Europe, they created an innovative solution which could have alleviated the debt impasse which was linked to the Debt Service Suspension Initiative (DSSI) and common framework initiative, (4) Saveshen has presented at the African Governance Seminar Series in Nairobi 2019 in which he presented solutions on how the private sector can collaborate with the public sector to alleviate some of the credit rating related solutions in Africa, (5) Saveshen has on numerous occasions attended and presented as an external expert at the African Union's ad hoc expert committee on credit rating agencies, (6) Credit Rating Analytics and Saveshen have partnered with senior faculty members at Harvard Business School for research which could pave the way for a better understanding of Africa's credit rating landscape.[1] The company has also recently contributed to the United Nations annual development report on Africa.[2] This report provided insights into how the SME credit rating concept can be used to proliferate funding opportunities within the supply chain finance space and increase transparency within this lending channel. Saveshen is a regular contributor on both digital and print media on the concept of credit ratings and has spoken widely about the credit rating industry as a whole and how it can be repositioned to better serve the needs of related stakeholders. Lastly, Saveshen serves as an independent director at a subsidiary of one of the world's largest credit rating agencies.[3]

[1] Pillay, Saveshen, and Anywhere Sikochi. "The Credit Rating Agency Market in Africa." Harvard Business School Working Paper, No. 22-074, June 2022. (Journal of Financial Reporting, proposal accepted-in-principle).

[2] United Nations. (2023). Economic Development In Africa Report. [Online]. United Nations. Available at: https://unctad.org/system/files/official-document/aldcafrica2023_en.pdf [Accessed 31 August 2023].

[3] At the time of writing, Saveshen serves as an independent non-executive director at Care Ratings South Africa, its parent company, The Care Edge Group, is estimated to be the largest rating agency outside of the big three—this is in terms of the number of outstanding/completed rating assignments.

Abbreviations

$	amounts are in US Dollars
AFCTA	African Continental Free Trade Area
BDF	Banque de France
CBIRC	China Banking and Insurance Regulatory Commission
CSRC	China Securities Regulatory Commission
ECB	European Central Bank
EMs	Emerging Markets
ESG	Environmental, Social and Governance
ESMA	European Securities and Markets Authorities
FIBEN	FIchier Bancaire des Entreprises
G-20	Group of Twenty Countries
GDP	Gross Domestic Product
GNP	Gross National Product
ICAS	In-house Credit Assessment System
IFC	International Financial Corporation
JSE	Johannesburg Stock Exchange
MSME	Micro, Small, and Medium Enterprises
nMSMEs	nano, Micro, Small, and Medium Enterprises
NAFMII	National Association of Financial Market Institutional Investors
NBFI	Non-Bank Financial Institutions
NCBs	National Central Banks
NDRC	National Development and Reform Commission
NFCs	Non-Financial Companies
NPL	Non-Performing Loans
OECD	The Organisation for Economic Co-operation and Development

PBOC	People's Bank of China
PD	Probability of Default
SCF	Supply Chain Finance
SIDBI	Small Industrial Development Bank of India
SME	Small and Medium Enterprises
SMEDAN	Small Medium Enterprise Development System of Nigeria
SMERA	Small and Medium Enterprise Rating System
SOCs	State-Owned Companies
SOEs	State-Owned Enterprises
SPV	Special Purpose Vehicle
SWOT	Strengths, Weaknesses, Opportunities, and Threats
vSMEs	very small, Small, and Medium Enterprises
WBG	The World Bank Group

List of Figures

List of Tables

1

Introduction

As we navigate through a post-COVID-19 environment, governments worldwide are placing a major emphasis on small and medium enterprises (SMEs) and actively crafting strategies to revive this integral sector. SMEs are generally the largest contributors to economic growth and employment in developed and developing economies. A major focus has been on the perennial issue of access to finance, but there has also been a concerted effort to enhance their inherent competitiveness in an effort to boost exports.[1] Whilst governments have made a substantial effort on this front, a large number of interventions have had a limited effect on alleviating these issues. SME credit ratings, which are a largely nebulous and underutilised concept, have proven to be an effective tool to both proliferate the global competitiveness of SMEs and enhance their ability to access funding opportunities. These ratings are a fairly new concept in the context of traditional credit ratings and thus remain unknown within most countries. For example, with the funding challenges on the African continent, just a handful of SME credit rating agencies have a comprehensive SME credit rating offering.[2] This trend persists globally as roughly 40 organisations are providing these services across all markets; the figure is relatively low when we consider that there are approximately 150

[1] Many emerging market countries experience a shortage of USD reserves, and increased exports from the SME sector can alleviate this issue.

[2] There is just a single SME credit rating agency providing a comprehensive SME credit rating offering on the African continent. Other organisations provide related services to SMEs but these are often in the form of SME due diligence, which are similar but differ from a technical perspective.

S. Pillay, *The Next Frontier in SME Ratings*,
https://doi.org/10.1007/978-3-031-54015-8_1

traditional credit rating agencies.[3] Thus, this industry is in its infancy stage but provides a much-needed service based on the benefits these ratings can provide. An interesting observation that is discussed in detail within the latter chapters is the public sector SME rating model, which has been met with high levels of success in Europe. The public sector credit rating model, in general, has garnered a lot of attention in the aftermath of the global financial crisis. However, many unsuccessful attempts have been made to establish a public sector entity focusing on traditional credit ratings.[4] On the other hand, the public sector SME credit rating model has been shown to be quite effective. This book offers comprehensive insights into the public sector model and provides a roadmap for countries interested in leveraging their SME industries to drive economic development. The author's company, Credit Rating Analytics, is currently assisting an emerging market government in creating the world's largest public sector grading agency, and some of the project's observations are shared within this book.[5] Due to the limited number of public sector SME credit rating agencies, the insights from the chapters covering this concept can be valuable to governments keen on establishing similar entities. There are additional ancillary services which are linked to the public sector SME credit rating concept, such as the SME loan mediation service, which has been a valuable tool for overturning unfavourable credit rating decisions. We unpack these ancillary services and highlight how they can be used to complement and enhance the SME credit rating concept.[6]

Lastly, we provide recommendations on how a private sector credit rating industry can be established either in isolation or concurrently with a public sector industry. We introduce innovative concepts such as the private sector ecosystem model, which is a collective effort by various stakeholders in which the credit rating concept is promoted to improve access to credit. Although these ratings have proven to be highly effective amongst SMEs, the services are not widely available, and the SME rating concept, in general, has largely

---

[3] The big three rating agencies, S&P, Moody's, and Fitch, are often quoted; however, there are many smaller credit rating agencies.

[4] Traditional credit ratings involve rating sovereigns, corporates, financial institutions, derivative-backed securities, and related securities or projects.

[5] Credit Rating Analytics is currently the lead advisor to an emerging market government on the establishment of the world's largest public sector grading agency, which focuses exclusively on nano, micro, small, and medium enterprises. A grading agency is similar to a rating agency but focuses on measuring the relative performance of businesses within a sector. These gradings are used to open up business opportunities but can also complement the lending process.

[6] We focus on these ancillary services within the subsequent chapters and showcase how the SME credit rating concept complements these services.

not taken off in most regions.[7] This book then provides policy recommendations on how these industries can be kick-started and how the value proposition can be adjusted so that the ratings better serve the needs of all related stakeholders. We will attempt to reduce the information gap that is associated with the concept and provide readers with a thorough understanding of SME ratings. The ultimate objective is to increase the availability of these ratings and improve both access to credit and business opportunities for the sector that is the backbone of most economies around the world.

[7] The author believes that this is due to the limited awareness of the concept and that the value proposition is not properly aligned with the borrowing requirements of SMEs.

Part I

An Overview of the SME Industry

Section One provides a comprehensive overview of the current state of the SME industry, delving into its prospects in a post-COVID-19 environment. Over the past few years, the SME sector has faced immense challenges, and we analyse both its historical performance and projected performance. Additionally, this section explores key SME-related themes, such as access to finance and market opportunities, which are integral to the SME credit rating concept. By examining these concepts in detail, we lay a solid foundation for the book, demonstrating how the SME credit rating concept can address and mitigate the pressing issues affecting this vital sector.

2

An Overview of the SME Industry

2.1 The Importance of the SME Industry and its Economic and Socioeconomic Contributions to Both Developed and Emerging Markets

The micro, small, and medium enterprise (MSME) or small and medium enterprise (SME) industries are generally the most critical contributors to economic output, socioeconomic development, and the creation of new jobs in both developed and developing economies. The economic catastrophe that occurred during the COVID-19 pandemic, which stemmed from the negative effect on MSMEs/SMEs, was a clear indication of the importance of this business segment. These businesses serve as the backbone of economic activity and should play a prominent role in the economic recovery in a post-COVID-19 environment. Governments throughout the world have made a concerted effort to revive this sector, and major multilaterals have shared this sentiment.[1] It can, however, be argued that many of these efforts have had a minimal impact, as a large number of SMEs have not managed to recover and remain out of business. Nevertheless, governments continue on an unrelenting pursuit of trying to bolster this pivotal sector due to its importance to the overall economic system.

[1] The IFC, for example, has placed SME development at the forefront of its mandate and is involved in multiple projects aimed at alleviating the issues facing this sector.

S. Pillay, *The Next Frontier in SME Ratings*,
https://doi.org/10.1007/978-3-031-54015-8_2

Before continuing, and due to the book's intended international audience, it is worth pointing out that the definition of an SME varies across different jurisdictions. For example, a micro-enterprise in Europe or North America might be considered a small enterprise in Africa. As an important reference point, Table 2.1 provides an overview of the classification of MSMEs, which is based on an average classification across different regions.[2] As turnover varies significantly across geographies, reference is also made to the number of employees, total assets, and loan size at origination. The actual classification within countries might vary significantly; for example, some countries might have a cut-off point for medium enterprises at 100 employees and some at 500 employees.[3]

Within Table 2.1, an MSME would need to obtain two of the three criteria within the definition section or if the origination loan falls within the loan thresholds on the right. It should be noted that many countries might differ in their classification of the SME/MSME industry, and there might be further segregation at the industry level. For example, the agricultural sector within a particular country might have a different definition criterion relative to the manufacturing sector. We will refer to Table 2.1 as a collective classification reference point. To simplify things, we will utilise the term SME for large parts of the book when referring to SME credit ratings and will reference

Table 2.1 The classification of SMEs/MSMEs across various jurisdictions

The Entity would need to meet two of the three criteria				
	Employees	Total Assets	Annual Sales	Loan Size at origination
Micro	0–9	< $1,00,000	$50,000–$2,50,000	< $10,000
Small	10–49	$1,00,000–$3,000,000	$2,50,001–$3,000,000	< $1,00,000
Medium	50–300	$3,000,000–$15 000 000	$3,000,001–$15,000,000	$1,000,000–$2,000,000

*Some countries do a further segregation within the micro-enterprise sector whereby the nano category is included. The nano category includes extremely informal businesses with low levels of turnover and a low number of employees (usually one); it is used from a policy perspective to better segregate the micro sector and allow for targeted interventions[4]

Source IEG (2019)

[2] The classification above is one of the classification criteria that the World Bank group utilises; however, different divisions within the World Bank Group might use different classifications.

[3] Some countries also focus predominantly on the number of employees and introduce turnover when there is no clarity on how to classify enterprises using only the number of employees.

[4] Nigeria is one of the countries to introduce this category as they have one of the world's largest numbers of nano enterprises. Adding the classification allows them to formulate interventions which are directly targeted at this segment.

MSMEs where needed.[5] However, irrespective of the classification method used, it is common knowledge that the SME sector is a major contributor to economic and socioeconomic development. The World Bank estimates that SMEs make up 90% of all businesses globally, 50% of all employment, and create roughly 70% of all new jobs.[6] This market segment is also a major contributor to overall GDP within most countries and will play a significant role in the future development of many emerging and frontier countries over the coming decades. By 2030, roughly 3.3 million new jobs will be required each month in emerging markets to absorb the growing workforce, and this sector will play an integral role in employing these job seekers.

From a socioeconomic perspective, SMEs are a major source of employment within both developing and developed countries. Poor economic conditions and limited job opportunities have forced many individuals into entering the challenging world of entrepreneurship, which serves as an indirect safety net and opportunity to participate in the economy.[7] The COVID-19 pandemic, which resulted in the closure of many businesses, also resulted in the creation of new ones due to many individuals being laid off from formal employment and taking up the entrepreneurship route out of necessity and desperation. The pandemic has allowed individuals to reassess working conditions, their personal objectives, and future ambitions, resulting in many gravitating towards the flexible nature of entrepreneurship. The economic recovery will determine how this trend plays out, as the initial operating years of SMEs are often challenging.[8] A recent study by the World Economic Forum indicates that 67% of executives from SMEs highlight survival and expansion as their main challenges.[9] From an employment

[5] Chapter four provides insights into how these ratings can also cater specifically to the micro-enterprise sector.

[6] World Bank. (2023). Small and Medium Enterprises (SMEs) Finance. [Online]. World Bank. https://www.worldbank.org/en/topic/smefinance (Accessed 26 July 2023).

[7] In many countries, this remains the only avenue to participate in the economy as there are limited or no formal employment opportunities.

[8] The survival rate of SMEs varies across the world and is exceptionally high in some jurisdictions; for example, in South Africa, around 70–80% of SMEs fail within the first 5-years which is one of the highest rates: Friedrich, C. (2023). Why do approximately 70–80% of small businesses fail within five years? [Online]. University of the Western Cape. https://www.uwc.ac.za/news-and-announcements/news/how-can-south-african-entrepreneurs-succeed-897 (Accessed 13 August 2023).

In countries such as the US, this figure is slightly lower, whereby roughly 20% fail in the first year and about 48% fail after 5 years. Lendingtree. (2023). The Percentage of Businesses That Fail—and How to Boost Your Chances of Success. [Online]. Lendingtree. https://www.lendingtree.com/business/small/failure-rate/ (Accessed 14 September 2023).

[9] Rajah & Woeffray. (2022). Future Readiness of SMEs and Mid-Sized Companies: A Year On. [Online]. World Economic Forum. https://www3.weforum.org/docs/WEF_Future_Readiness_of_SMEs_and_Mid_Sized_Companies_A_Year_On_2022.pdf (Accessed 13 September 2023).

perspective, SMEs are major contributors; however, their contributions vary by country and business size (Fig. 2.1).

Apart from the broader socioeconomic benefits, the industry is a key enabler for marginalised and underrepresented groups to participate in the economy. For example, females in many developed and developing countries lack equal employment opportunities, and entrepreneurship provides a platform to emancipate themselves economically (Figs. 2.2 and 2.3).

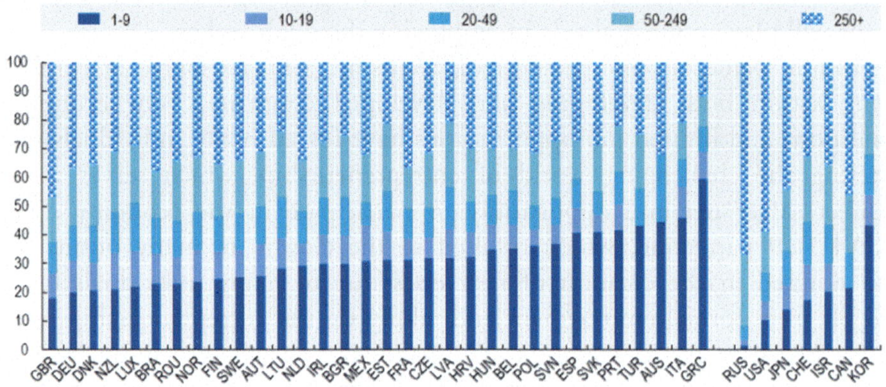

Fig. 2.1 The percentage of all persons employed within the SME segment (*Source* OECD [2017])

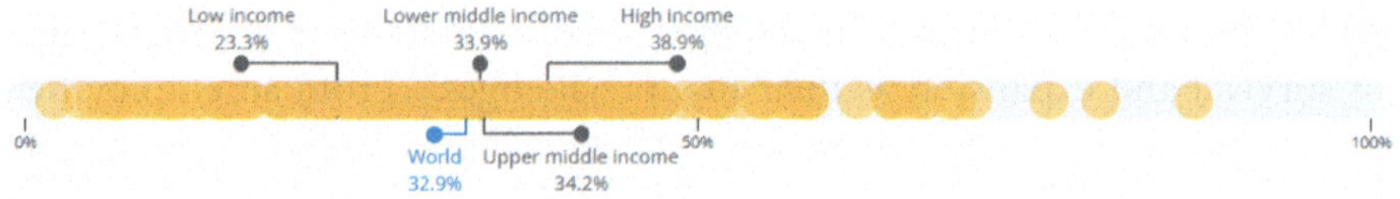

Fig. 2.2 Firms with female participation in ownership (*Source* World Bank, Enterprise Surveys)

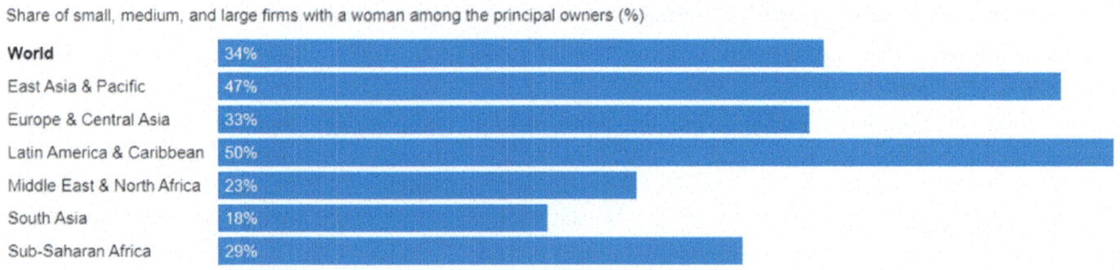

Fig. 2.3 Globally, just 1 in 3 businesses are female-owned (*Source* World Bank Gender Data Portal)

A portion of the female-owned SME segment prefers the flexibility that is associated with the entrepreneurship route, as it allows them to simultaneously focus on family-related matters, which is difficult when employed on a full-time basis. Due to the large number of low-skilled employees the industry hires, it plays an important role in upskilling them via skill development and educational programs. Additionally, employment within the SME sector provides healthcare and other social benefits that provide a safety net to these employees and have knock-on effects on overall socioeconomic development.[10] The SME industry also houses many social enterprises that are pivotal in addressing socioeconomic imbalances by implementing and creating solutions to alleviate these issues. Furthermore, these social enterprises have grown to contribute significantly to overall GDP and employment due to the large number of social issues which need to be addressed.[11] The prominent emergence of the ESG theme has brought many of these social issues to the forefront, and social enterprises have been notable contributors to innovative policy development. SMEs will play a central role in the transition to green energy solutions by providing related goods and services, which, in turn, reduces their overall carbon footprint. For example, in the UK, SMEs are responsible for over 90% of clean technology businesses.[12] These entities will then play a prominent role in the transition to green energy and should be supported to maximise their positive benefits on this front. The concept of SME ESG ratings, which is unpacked later in this book, will be integral in assisting SMEs in addressing some of these issues.

[10] Whilst SMEs might not directly provide these benefits in most instances, employment provides the financial means to access these important benefits.

[11] In the UK, social enterprises contribute £60 billion to GDP and employ roughly 2,000,000 people: Barclays. (2021). Barclays and Social Enterprise UK report a record-breaking rise in the number of social enterprises. [Online]. Barclays. Available at: https://home.barclays/news/press-releases/2021/10/barclays-and-social-enterprise-uk-report-a-record-breaking-rise-/#:~:t (Accessed 3 October 2023).

[12] OECD. (2017). Meeting of the OECD Council at Ministerial Level. [Online]. OECD. https://www.oecd.org/industry/C-MIN-2017-8-EN.pdf.

2.2 An Overview of the Existing Challenges that SMEs Encounter with Access to Funding Opportunities and the Effects of this on the Sustainability of these Businesses

The perennial challenge of access to funding is a common issue in both developed and developing economies. The issue has been at the forefront of government initiatives related to the SME sector; however, many of these response mechanisms have had a tenuous effect. The World Bank Group estimates that roughly 65 million enterprises, or 40% of formal micro, small, and medium enterprises, have an annual unmet financing gap of roughly $5,2 trillion.[13] Of this $5,2 trillion financing gap, $4,5 trillion is attributable to SMEs, with $718.8 billion being attributable to micro-enterprises. The current demand for credit within the MSME space sits at $8.9 trillion, with the supply of credit being a mere $3.2 trillion, resulting in an overall unmet demand of 59% or $5,2 trillion.

As per Fig. 2.4, when examining the unmet finance gap in greater detail, we find that micro-enterprises have a larger funding gap relative to their demand at 81%.[14] Small and medium enterprises, on the other hand, although having a larger aggregate financing gap in absolute terms, have a much lower financing gap in percentage terms, at 56%. The formal nature of SMEs, their size, and the profile of their businesses are contributing factors to this. It is also important to note that small businesses receive 96% of all funding that is provided to the MSME sector. Nevertheless, the overall funding gap is still notably large, resulting in it being a central area of focus for multilateral organisations and the public sector. Figure 2.5 provides an overview of the funding gap across all countries globally:

The graphic above provides a heat map of the severity of the funding gap across various emerging market regions. The source of these issues is multifaceted (discussed in Tables 2.2 and 2.3) and has been exacerbated by the COVID-19 pandemic.

Apart from the issues mentioned above, a lack of government and central bank support in some regions has proven to be a significant impediment to access to finance. This is predominantly based on interventions that can be

[13] IFC. (2017). MSME FINANCE GAP. [Online]. World Bank Group. https://www.smefinanceforum.org/sites/default/files/Data%20Sites%20downloads/MSME%20Report.pdf (Accessed 26 July 2023)].

[14] Micro-enterprises have a total credit demand of $882 billion of which just $163,2 billion has been met.

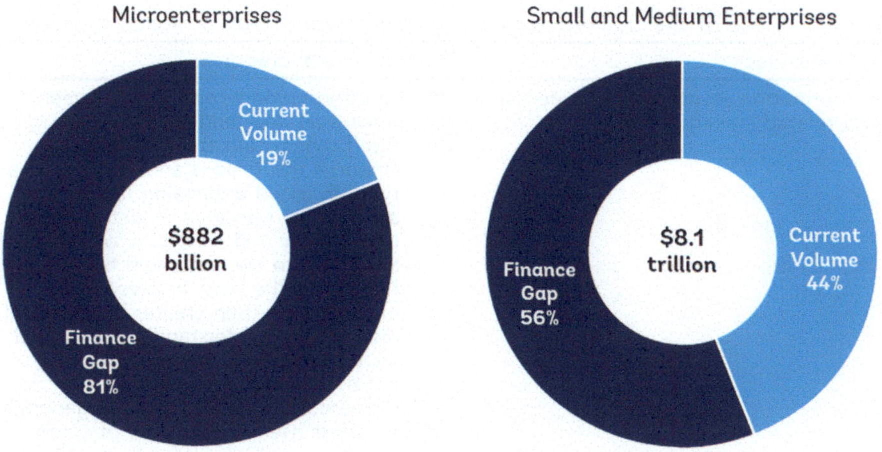

Fig. 2.4 An overview of the finance gap affecting micro-enterprises and Small and medium enterprises (*Source* IFC [2017])

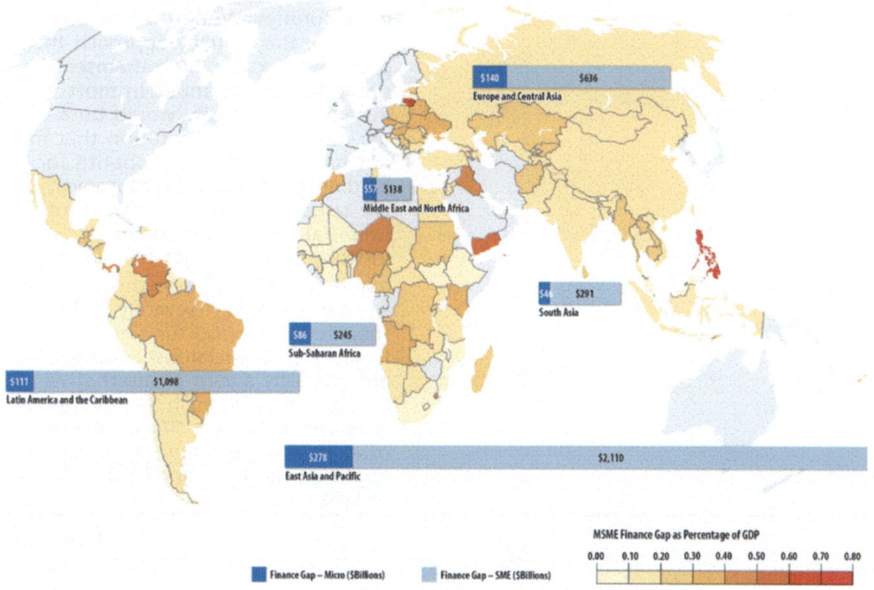

Fig. 2.5 The severity of funding gaps across different regions (*Source* IFC [2017])

made and are made in some jurisdictions but are not being made in others. For example, the public sector SME rating model, prevalent in Europe, has significantly impacted access to finance within countries that have established these entities. The model has not been adopted outside of Europe, which can be viewed as a shortcoming of countries that have failed to do so. The same

Table 2.2 Some of the challenges that contribute to the issue of access to credit

Key challenges	Further elaboration
An information asymmetry between SMEs and related stakeholders	The information asymmetry between borrowers and lenders is quite significant within the SME space. Financial institutions and multinationals typically avoid dedicating large amounts of resources to determining the viability and credibility of individual SMEs due to the perceived benefits relative to the costs involved in this exercise. This then creates a significant distortion in understanding SMEs and increases the risk appetite of doing business with these entities. The increased risk appetite would generally manifest itself in the form of credit rejections or high interest rates[15]
Limit knowledge of and access to tier two lenders and alternative traditional lenders	SMEs are often focused on either surviving or growing their existing businesses and are not fully aware of the financial institutions that can assist them with accessing funding opportunities. When they require funding, they usually approach their primary bank and limit themselves to a single funding channel. In most instances, this entity would be a tier-one financial institution that might not have a significant appetite for lending to these SMEs. Moreover, SMEs are largely not in contact with other financial institutions or tier 2 institutions that might have a larger appetite for lending to them.[16] This is a major issue as it severely constricts their funding opportunities. Apart from traditional financial institutions, SMEs are not fully aware of alternative lending channels such as private equity, venture capital, etc. These channels offer innovative financing options that might be better aligned with the needs of SMEs

(continued)

[15] The primary value-add of an SME credit rating is to reduce this information gap, which is discussed extensively in subsequent chapters.

[16] SMEs might be aware that such organisations exist but might not have a clear idea of who they might be, how to contact them and if they have an appetite to lend to their business. They might also have the misconstrued opinion that if a large tier-one bank rejects their credit application, then there is a remote chance that it will be accepted by a smaller tier-two institution.

Table 2.2 (continued)

Key challenges	Further elaboration
Limited knowledge of newer, fast-growing industries and businesses by traditional lenders	Traditional lenders are sometimes limited in their understanding of newer, fast-growing industries, which can distort the perceived potential and risks inherent in these industries. These distortions negatively affect the ability of SMEs to access credit facilities, thereby curtailing their sustainability and long-term potential. As indicated above, other channels, such as private equity and venture capital, might have a greater appetite, but SMEs are unfamiliar with these funding options
Lower appetite due to higher perceived risks within the SME sector	The SME sector is generally perceived to carry higher levels of risk; whilst this is true in many instances and confirmed by historic default statistics, it is sometimes exaggerated due to the information asymmetry and a lack of understanding of these businesses
Exorbitant interest rates are charged to the SME industry	Securing credit is a significant challenge for SMEs, and once secured, the borrowing rates are quite high, which decreases the economic value-add of the borrowed funds. Predatory pricing by financial institutions is a common practice whereby the cost of credit is often not based on the inherent risks but rather on banks' pricing power.[17] Interest rate compression between large and small firms varies significantly across regions, and larger firms are frequently charged much lower rates. There are exceptions, such as France, which houses the world's largest SME credit rating agency and simultaneously has one of the world's lowest interest compression rates[18]

(continued)

[17] Financial institutions have greater leverage over SMEs as they are aware that SMEs have limited options when it comes to funding opportunities. It should also be noted that banks have credit policies which restrict SMEs from obtaining credit if they are newly banked clients. This then further restricts funding opportunities when such practices are in place and can result in financial institutions having significantly more leverage over the interest rates charged to the SME sector.

[18] Banque de France has an SME credit rating unit, which is discussed extensively later. We quote the interest rate compression and compare this amongst other OECD countries.

Table 2.2 (continued)

Key challenges	Further elaboration
Short borrowing tenures	Short borrowing tenures are a key issue in which SMEs are only extended credit over short tenures. This is owing to the perceived risks that are associated with SMEs over the medium-long term. These short borrowing tenures then limit SMEs in terms of their ability to make long-term capital investments and have an inhibiting effect on their long-term development
A limited number of lending products are available to the SME sector	In instances when lending is available to the SME sector, the range of lending products is often limited, and it does not suit the needs of this sector. Sophisticated lending products available to large businesses are typically unavailable to portions of the SME segment that could benefit from such products
A limited understanding of available schemes proving lending assistance	There are currently many lending schemes and initiatives (generally by the public sector); however, the disaggregated nature of these initiatives makes it difficult for SMEs to be aware of the available schemes and how to access them. Knowledge of these schemes is also not provided at the initiation point of a lending request, resulting in many SMEs not using these potentially impactful schemes
The informal nature of SMEs	The informal nature of SMEs makes it difficult for financial institutions to want to lend to them as they generally lack proper financial record-keeping, which is typically a prerequisite for access to credit. Financial institutions often quote this as one of the leading inhibiting factors for SMEs seeking credit. The latter chapters introduce the SME credit rating concept and provide recommendations on addressing the issue of access to credit. A large percentage of the nano and micro-enterprise sector in most countries is informal in nature

can be said about the public sector SME loan mediation service, which is also concentrated in Europe and is not readily available in other jurisdictions.[19]

[19] The SME loan mediation service is a unique offering which was introduced by some countries in the aftermath of the global financial crisis and has proven to be extremely affective at overturning

Table 2.3 The challenges and hindrances that have constricted business opportunities

Key challenges	Further elaboration
Lacking third-party verification of the business and its capabilities	In instances where SMEs can properly articulate their capabilities, there are often challenges with regard to the authenticity of the data/claims put forward. This then creates doubt in the end users of these business profiles, which might affect the prospects of doing business. In these instances, contracting parties would be more comfortable if a third party independently verified the business and provided an in-depth evaluation of the business prospects and capabilities going forward
Difficulty in getting large corporate clients to incorporate SMEs into their supply chains and procurement practices	One of the key contributors to SMEs remaining within the "SME trap" is their inability to tap into the supply chain networks of larger clients.[20] A major contributor to this is the information asymmetry and poor understanding of SMEs. This stems from the costs and time involved in properly verifying an SME, which becomes difficult when there is limited information on these entities. Larger corporates might find it easier to do business with larger, more established entities with lower due diligence requirements. However, many of these larger corporations would do business with SMEs if there was easily accessible due diligence reporting from a reputable source
Finding it difficult to secure export orders with both regional, continental, and international clients	Another contributor to remaining within the "SME trap" is the inability of SMEs to secure export orders and expand their client base. The inability to diversify into additional client bases and tap into extra revenue sources can be viewed as a major inhibitor to an SME's long-term development and sustainability. Third-party verification has proven to be effective in assisting SMEs in securing these export orders; however, a lack of such verification creates doubt amongst potential clients of these businesses. This is a common issue in most countries as SMEs make up a fraction of overall exports, apart from exceptions such as China, whereby SMEs make up in excess of 60% of exports[21]

(continued)

[20] The SME trap is a scenario in which a small business fails to transition into a medium-sized enterprise or if a medium enterprise fails to transition into a large enterprise and out of the SME segment altogether.

[21] OECD. (2022)., *Financing SMEs and entrepreneurs 2022: An OECD Scoreboard*. OECD Publishing, Paris. https://doi.org/10.1787/e9073a0f-en.

Table 2.3 (continued)

Key challenges	Further elaboration
Limited business development and marketing skills	SMEs are generally quite specialised in developing their goods and services but are sometimes lacking in other key business areas such as marketing and business development. The typical human capital constituent of micro and small enterprises (which makes up the majority of firms within the SME category) generally does not include a separate business development and marketing team. This function is handled by the business owner, who might not have the requisite skill set to conduct such activities. These SMEs then struggle to create structured and credible business profiles that clearly outline their firms' technical, financial, operational, and strategic capabilities.[22] Potential clients who might want to extend large contracts to SMEs would need such information to determine if these businesses can undertake such orders

The lack of similar interventions by governments outside of these jurisdictions can be viewed as a contributing factor that has negatively affected SMEs' ability to access funding opportunities. The SME rating concept, which forms the basis of this book, is a key enabler in alleviating many of the access to finance issues mentioned above, and the subsequent chapters outline how the concept can be made more widely available.

2.3 An Overview of the Ability of SMEs to Access New Business Opportunities, the Segment's Contribution to Exports, and Why these Entities Struggle with Global Competitiveness

Separate from the perennial issue of access to finance, access to market is another critical issue that SMEs struggle with, and this is a major inhibitor to both sustainability and long-term development. It can be argued that even if funding opportunities were readily available, this would not automatically

unfavourable credit decisions. We refer to the concept as being an ancillary service to the SME credit rating concept and also discuss how this concept can be brought to fruition.

[22] Some businesses might be in a position to do so but there might be questions around the authenticity of the content as a credible third-party firm has not verified it.

translate into increased revenue or business success.[23] This is evident in many markets where special funding initiatives are created; however, this does not result in flourishing and sustainable SMEs nor a positive economic value-add from this sector. Increased market opportunities can then be viewed as one of the other main contributors to the viability and growth of SMEs. Government responses targeted at business development activities have been a mechanism by which to address this issue and have become prevalent in many countries. Some of the pertinent issues that impede business opportunities are highlighted in Table 2.3.

The factors explored in Table 2.3 apply to SMEs in both developed and developing countries and are a major stumbling block that inhibits SMEs from doing business with other SMEs and larger firms. However, some of the issues prohibiting access to market might be linked to deeper structural issues such as a lack of skills, educational systems with little emphasis on entrepreneurship, creativity, and infrastructure deficiencies. These structural issues cannot be addressed by the solutions put forward within this book; however, they should be noted as they are significant and a major inhibiting factor.

2.3.1 Access to Market, Exports, and Global Competitiveness

Regarding regional and international markets, SMEs typically participate via direct exports, indirect exports, non-equity contractual agreements, foreign direct investment, and fast-developing technological platforms. We focus on exports within this section due to its direct link to SME credit ratings, which creates a necessary foundation for the chapters ahead. Exports (both direct and indirect) are the most effective way in which SMEs can participate globally and, in doing so, provide significant knock-on benefits to these firms. For example, exporting has been shown to boost profitability by up to 26%; productivity and innovation would also naturally improve to cater for increased competition from other markets, and there would be an increase in employment within exporting firms.[24] With regard to contributions to global value chains, SMEs can contribute to this via direct exports or indirectly via their value chain contributions to other exporting firms. The percentage of

[23] Many wealthy countries experienced this issue in which there are numerous funding schemes, guarantee schemes, and direct government intervention; however, this does not automatically translate into growth in the SME sector.

[24] Atkin, D., & Jinhage, A. (2017). Trading up: The benefits of exporting for small firms. IGC, Growth Brief Series 011. London: International Growth Centre.

overall exports of final goods and services that stem from the SME sector varies between countries, regions, and levels of development. On an aggregate basis, SMEs are responsible for 33% of exports from selected developed countries and 18% from selected developing countries.[25] However, there are outliers within the above figures, such as China, in which SMEs contribute a sizeable 68% of exports.[26] These figures are low and showcase the major opportunity for SMEs to diversify their existing revenue streams and boost the overall economic output of their respective countries.

Although SMEs play a significant role in overall economic activity and are actively involved at different stages of the supply chain process, their limited activity with direct exports is often linked to their competitiveness, particularly at a global level. This is owing to many factors and has major economic implications for most emerging market economies. Countries with limited levels of global competitiveness typically struggle with a shortage of dollar reserves and experience external vulnerabilities that have major implications, such as increases in foreign currency debt, currency weakness, and fiscal deterioration. It can, however, be argued that some of the shortcomings related to global competitiveness are not entirely structural in nature but are rather owing to other factors ranging from limited awareness of the goods and services from these smaller firms, a lack of due diligence on these SMEs, to lack of confidence from prospective international clients that want to do business with these entities. The Facebook-OECD-World Bank Future of Business survey highlighted some of these challenges; this study aimed to identify trade barriers, and survey participants with a digital presence highlighted the following challenges.[27]

- 63% had an issue with finding business partners,
- 41% cited market limitation challenges,
- 38% found different regulations to be a challenge,
- 35% pointed to customs regulations,
- 33% indicated that cultural and language barriers were a challenge,
- 31% had issues securing export finance,

[25] López González, J., & S. Sorescu. (2019, November 9). Helping SMEs internationalize through trade facilitation. OECD Trade. Policy Papers, No. 229, OECD Publishing, Paris. http://dx.doi.org/10.1787/2050e6b0-en.

[26] OECD. (2022)., *Financing SMEs and entrepreneurs 2022: An OECD Scoreboard*. OECD Publishing, Paris. https://doi.org/10.1787/e9073a0f-en.

[27] Facebook/OECD/World Bank. (2020). The Future of Business Survey. https://dataforgood.fb.com/global-state-of-smb.

- 29% stated poor online payment alternatives to sell online,
- 26% indicated that the large geographical distance from their home country was an issue,
- 18% had an issue with a poor internet connection to sell online.

As per the study quoted above, finding business partners was cited as a major challenge by the majority of respondents. One of the contributing factors to this is likely owing to the fact that businesses are reluctant to do business with foreign entities that they know little about and which have not been independently verified. This is to the detriment of SMEs who might have an equally compelling value proposition, but these entities are either unknown or, if they are, there is no third-party verification on their businesses. Apart from the above-mentioned issues, access to finance is also seen as a major contributing factor to constricted competitive advantages and limited export activity. This stems from the fact that global competitiveness at its very core is linked to technological innovations and related relative advantages. Obtaining these technological advantages is heavily linked to capex expenditure, which is often not permissible when access to finance remains a major challenge. Solving the issue of access to finance could then be seen as one of the enabling steps that would address the issue of limited exports, and within the later chapters of this book, we introduce the concept of SME ratings, which addresses both of these issues.

2.3.2 Remaining within the SME/MSME/nMSME (nano, Micro, Small, and Medium Enterprise) Trap

The SME/MSME trap is a situation in which an SME/MSME remains routed in their business classification segment and struggles to grow out of it. For example, businesses within the micro-enterprise segment might struggle to transition into the small business segment, or small businesses might struggle to transition into the medium-sized category.[28] This transition is an area of concern for governments as failure to do this results in some businesses remaining informal and limits their overall value-add to the economy. If we expand the micro-enterprise criteria to include nano enterprises,[29] this issue remains more pronounced and impedes the overall development of a country. It also negatively affects the government's tax collection capabilities as these

[28] Some businesses may be content with their level of development, but many entrepreneurs want to transition into the larger segments but might be constricted by external forces.

[29] Sometimes also referred to as very small enterprises or VSEs.

nano and micro businesses are generally non-tax paying entities, predominantly operating on a cash basis. Within the smaller business segments, both access to credit and access to market are challenges; however, access to market remains a larger contributing factor that anchors these entities within the nano and micro-enterprise categories.

The SME trap persists within both the small and medium enterprise sectors and prevents small businesses from transitioning into the medium enterprise category and medium enterprises from altogether transitioning out of the SME classification. Whilst businesses within the small business category are mostly formal entities, a larger portion might not be living up to their full potential from a value-add perspective, and a portion might also not be tax compliant.

In contrast to the micro-enterprise sector, small businesses would have larger borrowing requirements.[30] Businesses in this segment would typically struggle with access to market to some degree, and these challenges might be linked to their ability to access credit facilities. This is owing to the fact that in order to complete large orders, some sort of funding mechanism might be required. It is particularly relevant for export orders and is one of the reasons why small businesses struggle to secure exports. In terms of medium-sized enterprises, these entities are already doing significant amounts of business locally; however, regional and international exports might be a challenge. Medium-sized enterprises have existing credit lines with major financial institutions, yet, access to market opportunities might be limited due to an information asymmetry linked to their business and a lack of any sort of verification of their ability to fulfil export orders. From a growth and funding perspective, alternative funding vehicles might be required to transition these businesses into the large business segment. Non-traditional funding mechanisms such as private equity, private debt, and mezzanine finance have proven to be effective financing tools for proliferating development within the medium enterprise category. The SME rating concept, which is unpacked in the next chapter, is an important tool that can play an effective role in alleviating some of the issues associated with the "SME trap". For example, its ability to provide third-party verification and due diligence on businesses is a major value-add within the access to market space. This can be a mechanism to secure in-country business opportunities for micro-enterprises, in-country and regional opportunities for small businesses, and international export orders for medium enterprises. On the access to funding front, SME credit

[30] Small businesses may have business opportunities but might lack the requisite funding to execute some of these opportunities. This then naturally increases their borrowing requirement and might result in a larger funding requirement on a relative basis to the micro-enterprise segment.

ratings would play a major role in alleviating this issue as the concept has proven to be exceptionally effective at securing funding, decreasing interest rates, reducing collateral requirements, and increasing borrowing tenures. The next chapters then unpack the SME rating concept, its associated benefits, and suggestions on how the concept can be introduced in developed and developing countries.

References

IEG. (2019). *World Bank Group Support for Small and Medium Enterprises*. [Online]. World Bank Group. https://ieg.worldbankgroup.org/sites/default/files/Data/Evaluation/files/SME_Synthesis.pdf

IFC. (2017). *MSME FINANCE GAP*. [Online]. World Bank Group. https://www.smefinanceforum.org/sites/default/files/Data%20Sites%20downloads/MSME%20Report.pdf

OECD. (2017). Meeting of the OECD Council at Ministerial Level. [Online]. OECD. https://www.oecd.org/industry/C-MIN-2017-8-EN.pdf

The World Bank. (2023). Gender Data Portal. [Online]. The World Bank. https://genderdata.worldbank.org/ (Accessed 13 August 2023).

World Bank. (2023). Enterprise Surveys. [Online]. World Bank. Available at: https://www.enterprisesurveys.org/en/enterprisesurveys (Accessed 13 August 2023).

Part II

An Introduction to the SME Rating Concept

This section introduces the SME credit rating concept and outlines its development over the last two decades. The author provides a sequential breakdown of the growth of the industry across various regions, and we will also delve into the many factors that have impeded its development. We unpack some of the benefits of these ratings, which have been outlined in previous empirical studies, and will showcase the potential benefits of these ratings to alternative lending channels. A large number of these alternative lending channels currently operate without these ratings; however, stakeholder outcomes could be significantly optimised with the inclusion of the SME rating concept.

3

An Introduction to the "SME Rating", and Specific "SME Credit Rating" Concepts

3.1 What are SME Ratings?

SME ratings represent a broad category of underlying ratings created to decrease the information asymmetry between SMEs and contracting parties. The information asymmetry associated with SME ratings is the largest across all rating segments, and these ratings provide a comprehensive analysis of a particular business.[1] This then increases the willingness and propensity of contracting parties to do business with the rated entity due to a better understanding of the business. The SME rating industry, in general, is relatively new in the context of the entire credit rating industry, but the product offering has evolved to cater for the needs of multiple stakeholders that engage with SMEs.[2] Broadly speaking, these ratings can be broken up into the following categories (Table 3.1).

3.2 The History Behind the SME Rating Industry

From a traditional perspective, SME ratings were one of the first forms of ratings, dating back to North America in the 1800s. The industry traces its routes to the panic of 1837 when thousands of merchants failed to pay

[1] This is in comparison to sovereign, corporate, derivative, infrastructure, and project credit ratings.

[2] The traditional credit rating industry has been around over the past 100 years and can be viewed as a high-demand service offering.

S. Pillay, *The Next Frontier in SME Ratings*,
https://doi.org/10.1007/978-3-031-54015-8_3

Table 3.1 An overview of the different types of SME ratings

Type of rating	Further elaboration
SME Credit Ratings	SME credit ratings are the predominant form of SME ratings and have been created to decrease the information asymmetry between borrowers and lenders; the ratings can also be used as a hybrid due diligence tool. SME credit ratings are actively used in Asia, which currently has the largest private sector market in the world.[3] The concept is growing in Europe, comprising both a public and private sector market. These SME credit ratings are used to access credit via traditional channels such as banks and microlending organisations, as well as non-traditional channels such as SME debt exchanges and private debt markets
SME Due Diligence Ratings	The SME due diligence rating concept has been created to assist SMEs with access to market as it allows them to participate in the supply chain networks of larger firms and secure regional and international export orders. These ratings might exclude some of the complex financial ratios associated with credit ratings but are created to include information that will decrease the information asymmetry within business-to-customer and business-to-business transactions. SME credit ratings can be used as a due diligence tool, but some of the complicated data within these ratings might confuse end users of these reports. It should also be noted that although these ratings have not been created specifically for financing purposes, they can be used to complement funding activities. This is owing to the rating's ability to properly articulate the positioning of businesses, which is important to credit managers who might not have a clear understanding of these enterprises. These ratings are then quite versatile, and reporting is done so that a broad spectrum of end users can understand it SMEs can directly request these ratings or can be requested by third-party entities that need information on a particular enterprise. The rating process is largely similar to credit ratings; however, no rating scale is assigned to the rating but rather a broad analysis of the business. Due diligence ratings are particularly important for companies that want to do business with other businesses in foreign jurisdictions. A lack of such due diligence is one of the inhibiting factors to securing export orders, and these ratings can be a major enabler; we touch on this aspect as the book progresses

(continued)

[3] The private sector market is concentrated in India and Bangladesh, which have been using the concept extensively.

Table 3.1 (continued)

Type of rating	Further elaboration
SME Gradings	The SME grading concept can be defined as an offshoot of due diligence ratings but takes it a step further by providing a sector and industry-wide ranking of SMEs in relation to their financial, operational, strategic, and legal/compliance performance. These ratings then allow for comparisons across businesses to determine the best in class but also to provide a benchmark from which businesses can understand their shortcomings and strengths. SMEs have a broad sense of some of their shortcomings but might not have an idea of the extent of this on an industry-wide basis. The ratings can then be used as an important inward-looking optimisation tool The grading concept covers many sectors, some of which are important in emerging markets, with the potential to significantly enhance the outcomes of rated entities and related stakeholders. For example, education, real estate, and healthcare are three of the most essential investments consumers make or save towards in emerging markets.[4] Within real estate gradings, there is a focus on build quality, the SME's experience in completing similar developments, the financial capability of the developer to complete the project, and the prospects of the development post-completion. These gradings are a major value-add as investors can assess the gradings of all real estate developers and then make informed decisions based on the detailed information provided to them. The gradings also provide a platform for best in class companies to showcase their capabilities and to be recognised and rewarded accordingly. If adopted broadly, these gradings have the potential to significantly improve the overall competitiveness of goods and services of SMEs within any country. When a public sector body hands out these gradings, the government could construct the methodologies to align with international standards. This, for example, improves the build quality of real estate developments and possibly attracts foreign investors due to overall improvement in standards. The same can be true for the educational sector, as many SMEs provide tertiary education but have no formal ranking of their relative performance. Due to the vast number of tertiary providers, these gradings can be an effective tool to facilitate better decision-making and enhance the quality of education

(continued)

[4] SMEs make up a large percentage of the overall service providers within these three important sectors. Within education, SMEs make up a large portion of early childhood development, and there is no actual ranking of relative performance within this important sector. When we look at healthcare, SMEs generally make up a large portion of medical centres, which is a preferred source of healthcare for many individuals.

Table 3.1 (continued)

Type of rating	Further elaboration
SME Bank Loan Ratings	SME bank loan ratings are used predominantly for regulatory purposes and are anchored on measuring the probability of default. The ratings are assigned to a particular credit facility and are constantly monitored and updated. The ratings are widely used in Asia and in countries that have adopted the standardised approach to measuring banks' credit exposures. These ratings can provide capital relief to banks, which can be passed on to SMEs in the form of increased lending to these channels[5]
SME ESG Ratings	SME ESG ratings are a fairly new concept and have been introduced to measure the ESG profile of SMEs. The ratings can either be provided on a stand-alone basis or added to other SME ratings. Whilst measuring the ESG score of micro and small enterprises is difficult, the ratings can be useful to larger SMEs within the medium enterprise category. The ESG rating concept has gained momentum with larger enterprises, and there has been a massive push to have these ratings adequately regulated to boost both oversight and uniformity amongst ratings

back their debts, one of the first notable examples of the dangers of doing business without formal due diligence on counterparties.[6] Mr Lewis Tappen formed the Mercantile Agency in New York as a service to mitigate this information asymmetry by providing due diligence assessments of the credibility of businesses. The agency utilised feedback from key stakeholders of rated enterprises to determine their credibility, which resembled one of the first peer rating systems in the world. The agency eventually started publishing its ratings and merged with its main rival at the time, Bradstreet and Co., and after subsequent mergers, it resulted in the formation of Dun & Bradstreet, which is still in operation to this day.[7] This gave rise to other forms of credit reporting, such as credit bureaus, which have become supporting pillars of the overall financial industry. Dun & Bradstreet currently does not provide SME credit ratings but indirectly does so via affiliations with other third-party firms; the company is also active in the credit bureau business via TransUnion and related entities.

[5] The capital relief to banks is provided in a scenario whereby these ratings allow banks to better assess and then provide more appropriate risk weightings to their exposures relative to default or in-house risk weights that are assigned to these exposures. Banks are then able to lend out more capital, potentially increase their profitability, and allocate capital to the SME sector more efficiently.

[6] James, Norris, D., Dun, R. G., & Co. (1978). 1841–1900: The Development of Credit-Reporting in the Nineteenth Century. Greenwood Press.

[7] Dun & Bradstreet Corporation. (1991). Dun & Bradstreet and the Rise of Modern Business: A History of the Dun & Bradstreet Corporation. Dun & Bradstreet.

From a modern perspective and SME ratings in their current form, the industry dates its roots back to private ratings handed out by the big three rating agencies to large unlisted SMEs in instances where these organisations tapped into financial/private markets for capital raising initiatives. The exact start date then becomes challenging to determine as there is no specific value proposition for these services as they are handled on an ad hoc basis. However, if we consider organisations with specific SME credit rating value propositions, then the industry's origin can be traced back to Asia. The region has the largest concentration of private sector SME rating agencies, with SMERA being registered as one of the first stand-alone SME credit rating agencies both regionally and globally.[8] A large number of traditional rating agencies have, however, included specific SME ratings into their overall product offering to cater to market demand as well as due to structural and regulatory features/requirements.[9] In both India and Bangladesh, the standardised approach for counterparty credit risk exposures is utilised to a large extent by banks. This then promotes the use of external credit assessment providers, and banks often request that SMEs be rated or request these ratings directly from rating agencies. This, together with the Indian government's "Performance and Credit Rating Scheme for Micro and Small Enterprises", an initiative that ran from 2005 to 2018, resulted in major demand for these services and an increase in the availability of SME ratings from traditional rating agencies.

Within Africa, there are approximately 20 credit rating agencies on the continent, with just a handful having comprehensive SME credit rating value propositions in place. Metropol in Kenya was one of the first entities to create a comprehensive value proposition; the company set up its offering in 2007 with assistance from multilateral organisations keen on increasing SME credit rating coverage. Other African firms have attempted to follow suit, but these efforts have focused on SME scoring and SME due diligence ratings. There is significant potential for the SME rating industry within Africa due to the projected growth within this segment and the considerable credit gap that exists.[10] Credit Rating Analytics (the author's firm) is currently

---

[8] SMERA. (2023). About Us. [Online]. SMERA. https://www.smeraonline.com/newweb/index.php/about/#:~:text=We%20provide%20an%20unbiased%20opinion,S.

[9] Traditional rating agencies are entities that provide corporate, derivative, municipal and sovereign ratings. These are the predominant entities which have decided to enter the SME rating space by creating bespoke SME credit rating value propositions.

[10] SME scoring provides a brief overview of an SME; by the author's estimates, SME scoring provides just 15% of the information that is included within an SME credit rating report. It can be used as a basic due diligence tool which provides information to users who might want an overview of a firm or a confirmation that a third party has verified the business.

in the process of assisting a country in creating the first public sector rating agency in emerging markets, which will become the world's largest once it is fully operational. The public sector SME rating agency will complement existing regional trade blocs, and the subsequent chapters unpack this project in greater detail.

SME credit ratings are provided by the public and private sectors in Europe and mainly cater to formal SMEs. Due to the developed nature of financial systems in Europe, SME credit ratings can assist with both bank financing and capital market/non-traditional financing activities. The "mini-bond" market is an example of an alternative lending channel that allows SMEs to issue debt directly from capital markets. Although serving as an effective channel to facilitate funding activities, these minibond exchanges have not grown exponentially due to structural issues. There is a large information asymmetry on these minibond exchanges due to the nature of SMEs and the lack of SME credit rating coverage.[11] Inbonis was one of the private sector pioneers of the concept in Europe, with a certification from the European Securities and Market Authority (ESMA) certification. The big three rating agencies have always been active in Europe but have focused on rating large SMEs that require these ratings for public or private debt issuances. These rating agencies also indirectly participate in the SME space by providing backend credit risk solutions to financial institutions active in the SME lending space. The private sector is complemented by the public sector, which provides these ratings via many European central banks.[12] These central banks' SME credit rating units were created to serve as In-house Credit Assessment Systems (ICAS) and play a vital role in the Eurosystem collateral framework. The ratings are extended beyond the Eurosystem collateral framework and have been a primary enabling tool for SMEs to access both traditional and non-traditional funding options. All of these public sector rating agencies are not registered with the ESMA; however, Banque de France specifically applied for an exemption, which was granted to them based on the nature of their operations. Some of the incoming chapters of this book are dedicated to the public sector model, which showcases its effectiveness as well as how it can be adopted in other countries.

The credit rating industry within the Middle East continues to develop in line with financial market development in the region; however, there has been

---

[11] Altman, E. I., Esentato, M., & Sabato, G. (2018). Assessing the credit worthiness of Italian SMEs and mini-bond issuers. *Global.*
Finance Journal, 2017, 100450. https://doi.org/10.1016/j.gfj.2018.09.003.

[12] The public sector rating agencies operating in Europe are via the SME credit rating units at: Banco de Espana (BBK), Banque de France (BdF), Banca d'Italia (BdI), Banco de Portugal (BdP), Banka Slovenjie (BS), Deutsche Bundesbank (BBk) and Oesterreichische Nationalbank (OeNB).

little activity within the SME credit rating space. Some of the multilateral development agencies, such as the Khalifa Fund and Dubai Chamber, have SME credit rating divisions in place; however, this is exclusive to projects within these organisations. Many governments are emphasising access to finance within the SME space, which could result in the creation of private and public sector industries within the region. Like the Middle East, South America and the Caribbean contain only a limited number of rating agencies focusing on the SME sector. Many traditional rating agencies operate in South America, but these entities tend to focus on the traditional credit rating business. The large credit gap within South America's SME space, which the Inter-American Development Bank estimates at $1.8 trillion, is evidence of the need to develop an SME credit rating industry. There have, however, been attempts to explore the creation of an SME credit rating industry, and this should come to fruition once there is additional awareness around this concept.

Although North America is one of the pioneers behind the overall concept, the region has no robust SME credit rating industry. Information availability is, however, relatively high in the US, resulting in lower information asymmetries. SME credit scoring, which is a watered-down version of the SME credit rating concept, is available, and banks tend to have sophisticated internal credit rating capabilities. However, the SME loan rejection rate in the USA is still quite large (>30%) relative to other OECD countries, so there is an argument for creating a fully-fledged SME credit rating industry (Fig. 3.1).

Lastly, when viewed in totality, the SME credit rating industry is still in its infancy stage, having been around for just 20–25 years relative to the traditional credit rating industry, which has existed for more than a century. As with any industry, development generally takes time, coinciding with increased awareness of the concept. Although there have been some concerted efforts to increase the availability of these ratings, such as the Performance and Credit Rating Scheme in India, various factors have contributed to the limited availability of these ratings. Table 3.2 highlights some of these reasons[13]:

The tenuous availability of these ratings has been one of the drivers behind my desire to write this book, as I have an unrelenting desire to increase awareness of this important concept and positively impact SMEs. Awareness around SME ratings is gradually picking up, and major multilateral organisations such as the World Bank Group have dedicated resources to

[13] The Performance and Credit Rating Scheme in India was a government-led initiative in which subsidies were provided to SMEs to obtain credit ratings from private sector rating agencies in the country.

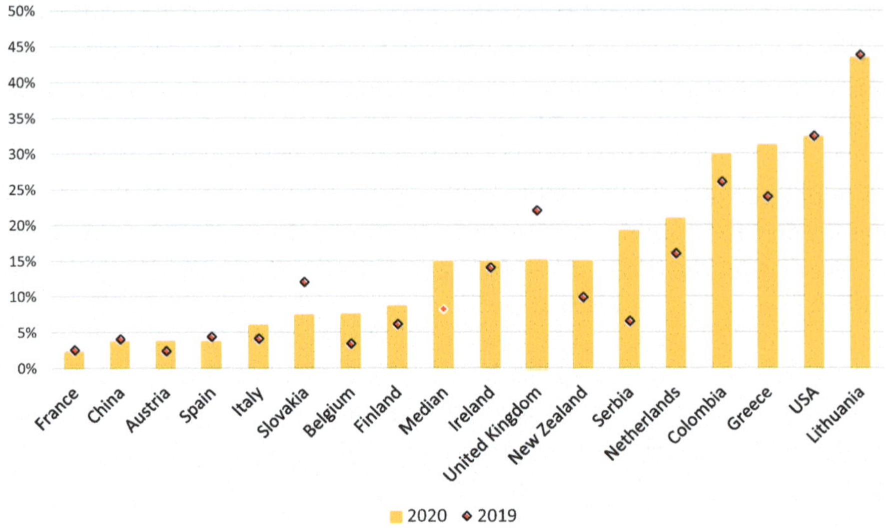

Fig. 3.1 The comparison of SME loan rejection rates amongst some of the large OECD countries (*Source* OECD [2022])

increasing the availability of these ratings. The recent project that Credit Rating Analytics completed for the International Finance Corporation is evidence of this, as the project was initiated to proliferate the development of this concept within emerging markets. Such interventions by key regional and continental development bodies could play a vital role in increasing the availability of these ratings. Furthermore, changes to the overall value proposition by making the ratings more impactful and addressing the core needs of SMEs are also necessary interventions that will naturally increase the use of these ratings. We explore this later and showcase how specific changes to the value proposition of rating agencies can significantly increase the demand for these services.

The section below provides an overview of the different SME rating agencies operating in various regions. An emphasis is placed on regions in which there are a large number of SME credit rating agencies to unpack what policies were in place to increase the availability of these ratings.

Table 3.2 Factors that have contributed to the slow development of the SME credit rating industry

Contributing factor	Further elaboration
Low levels of profitability within the SME credit rating industry	This has been one of the primary drivers behind the limited availability of these ratings. The traditional credit rating industry is one of the most profitable industries, and traditional rating agencies are the major players within the SME credit rating space. These organisations venture into the SME credit rating space to tap into an additional revenue stream but are often met with low levels of profitability, creating a reluctance to further expand their operations in this segment. The contributing factors to low levels of profitability are as follows: • The limited capacity of SMEs to pay for SME credit ratings • Limited awareness around the concept and low levels of demand lead to scale not being achieved • SMEs are generally reluctant to pay for a service that does not provide a guaranteed outcome Thus, traditional credit rating agencies have a proclivity to re-invest in the more profitable traditional credit rating space, leading to limited availability of SME ratings. The conventional credit rating industry is highly profitable, with many rating agencies showcasing profits in excess of 40%. The SME credit rating industry also requires significant scale to ensure profitability, which can only be achieved over time. Many rating agencies within the SME rating space or rating agencies wanting to enter this space are a bit reluctant to go through the initial loss-making years as their shareholders might not be that patient

(continued)

Table 3.2 (continued)

Contributing factor	Further elaboration
The informal nature of SMEs	A large number of SMEs within emerging markets are informal in nature, which makes it challenging to provide ratings to these entities. The primary issue stems from a lack of data availability, making it difficult to complete the rating process. A large number of these informal SMEs are also not keen on formalising themselves as they prefer operating under the radar and in a tax-free environment. These entities might not have a funding requirement due to the nature of their business and might not see value in getting rated. Within the project that Credit Rating Analytics is working on for an emerging market country, we have made a concerted effort to address this by introducing an SME credit rating preparation program. This program assists SMEs to reach the required formalisation level that would allow them to be rated. Addressing SMEs' informal nature is a key enabler to achieving widespread SME credit rating coverage
SME ratings are sometimes viewed as ineffective due to the structural dynamics within the SME lending space	SMEs require assistance from a borrowing perspective, both pre and post the rating process; however, in most instances, such assistance is not provided and results in unfavourable outcomes even after securing a credit rating. These businesses are typically single-banked, and a rated SME would have a better chance of securing funding if their rated profiles were shared with multiple funding partners. Within the traditional rating space, large or listed businesses receive assistance from corporate and investment banking teams, which source all potential lending options and use credit ratings to complement the lending process. The effectiveness of credit ratings in this setting might then be accentuated by these corporate and investment banking teams, resulting in credit ratings being perceived as being much more effective

(continued)

Table 3.2 (continued)

Contributing factor	Further elaboration
The cost sensitivity of SMEs	SMEs are naturally very cost-sensitive and are usually reluctant to part ways with their hard-earned revenue. It then becomes challenging to price these services at a level that makes financial sense to the rating agencies. The ratings have an underlying cost and typically require analyst input for the subjective variables; covering these costs and relaying this to consumers can be challenging. SMEs, particularly micro-enterprises, have struggled in a post-COVID-19 environment, and with many in survival mode, convincing them to pay for these ratings can be challenging. An alternative value proposition might be required to better appeal to SMEs, which is discussed in greater detail within the latter chapters
There is a lack of culture around using these ratings	Due to the concept being developed and made available over the past 20 years, there is a tenuous amount of culture around utilising these ratings. There are also limited marketing campaigns and capacity-building on this concept, which makes it unknown in most jurisdictions. Governments in most jurisdictions are unaware of this concept, and there is then little or no intervention on their part to grow the industry. Furthermore, individual SMEs are often unaware of the concept in the countries where these services are available. In most of these instances, centres of influence, such as accountants and lawyers, are unaware of the concept and thus unable to advise them to take up these services.[14] Even in countries such as India, where there was a concerted effort by the public and private sectors to drive the concept, there was still stagnation in the usage of these ratings due to a lack of awareness. However, it should be noted that culture takes time to build up, and the infancy stage of the overall industry is one of the key contributors to a lack of culture

(continued)

[14] A lack of strategically targeted awareness campaigns to these important stakeholders is one of the reasons behind this.

Table 3.2 (continued)

Contributing factor	Further elaboration
The SME financing industry has evolved to function without the need for these ratings	Although SME ratings are quite effective in achieving their intended purpose, the underlying financial industry has developed without these ratings, whereby the SME rating function has been indirectly outsourced. This is evident with microfinance organisations or bank intermediaries which obtain large credit facilities from traditional lenders and are tasked with: 1. Conducting extensive due diligence and effectively fulfilling the SME rating function 2. Adding on an interest rate premium and 3. On-lending to SMEs Markets have evolved in this way due to there initially being no structured SME rating function; changing this market dynamic then becomes a challenge and has contributed to the slow uptake of SME credit and due diligence ratings
Replicating the operating model utilised within the traditional credit rating industry	Replicating the traditional credit rating model has resulted in creating an SME credit rating model that is not aligned with the dynamics within the SME industry. For example, the conventional rating industry is largely human capital intensive, and this can be justified when we consider the high-profit margins or intricacy of these ratings. However, the low rating fees from the SME rating industry do not justify the human capital-intensive nature of the traditional rating model. Replicating this model then results in low or unprofitable margins within the SME credit rating space. To mitigate this, substantial investments in technology are required to decrease the amount of human intervention in the rating process; this requires large capital outlays, which some rating agencies are unwilling to make. Deploying the traditional operating model has thus resulted in inefficient outcomes, resulting in negative opinions around the profitability of this industry

3.3 A Mapping of the Global SME Credit Rating Industry (Including Existing Industry Players)

As previously discussed, the SME credit rating industry is still in its infancy stage, having been around for roughly two decades. Within this period, the industry has achieved modest growth anchored in Europe and Asia. The majority of SME rating activity is conducted by conventional credit rating agencies that have decided to roll out an SME credit rating offering. The infographic below provides an overview of some of the registered SME credit rating agencies (Fig. 3.2).

Figure 3.2 includes only SME rating agencies that are registered with the relevant authorities; although there has been a concerted effort to include all SME rating agencies, some might have been erroneously excluded. As per the infographic, European SME credit rating agencies are split between public and private sector companies; these sectors coexist but have slightly different operating models. The public sector rating agencies utilise an investor-pays model, and the private sector utilises either an issuer-pays or a hybrid model.[15] However, it is important to point out that the public sector model

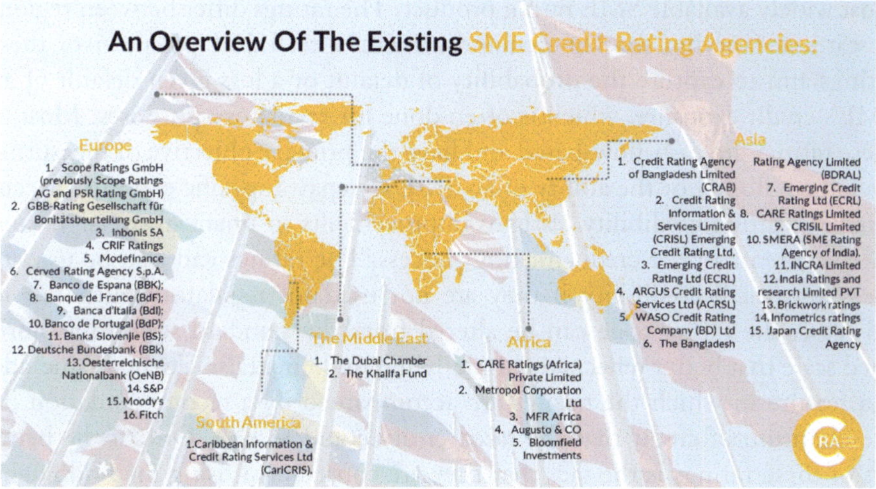

Fig. 3.2 A global mapping of existing SME credit rating agencies

---

[15] The issuer-pays model is the most commonly used within the credit rating industry and requires the issuer/borrower to pay a fee in order to get rated. The investor-pays model, on the other hand, requires that investors pay a subscription fee in order to obtain rating information, and a hybrid model is a combination of both models, which is also frequently used.

has managed to rate a larger portion of the overall SME market within the countries in which the model is adopted. For example, in France, the SME credit rating unit at Banque de France has managed to rate roughly 8% of the country's SMEs.[16] This is in contrast to the private sector SME credit rating agencies in India, which collectively rated a significantly smaller portion of the overall SME industry when the industry was at its peak of popularity and productivity.

3.4 An Introduction to the Technical Dynamics Behind these Ratings

This section will aim to highlight some of the technical features of these ratings, which will provide readers with a better understanding of the concept. To better understand these technical dynamics, it is important to unpack the different types of ratings, which are as follows:

3.4.1 SME Credit Ratings

As discussed earlier, the SME credit rating concept is the predominant and most widely available SME rating product. The ratings differ between regions to cater to varying market demands. From a technical perspective, these ratings aim to capture the probability of default or a loss given default of an SME's credit exposure, which is often done for regulatory purposes. Most of these ratings are cash-flow-based and have the primary objective of measuring overall credibility or the ability of an SME to repay a specific exposure. Accurately capturing credibility leads to improvements in financial oversight and enhancements in the credit-making process. The ratings can also be used to measure overall credibility if they are not used for regulatory purposes; in this case, the rating scale can be altered from the standard scale to a shortened scale that better reflects the underlying fundamentals. A major value-add is a feature in which the ratings are accompanied by a recommendation on the quantum of credit that the rated entity could receive. One of the benefits of these ratings is the fact that they are constructed using methodologies that cover a broad range of sectors and sub-sectors. This is viewed favourably by financial institutions, which typically have unidimensional methodologies which are not tailored to individual sectors. Approaching credit risk

[16] There are roughly 4,000,000 SMEs in France, with BDF managing to rate roughly 3,00,000 of them.

in this manner allows the rating agencies to model for default risk using industry-specific risk criteria. This results in a more accurate credit risk assessment, providing a differentiating value-add and creating a demand for such ratings. Another feature is that a typical SME credit rating report is highly comprehensive and includes the following content:

- A comprehensive breakdown of the history of the organisation and its ownership structure.
- Details related to the company's SME credit rating.
- Details related to the SME rating scale and how to interpret the rating scale.
- A thorough analysis of the operational capabilities of the SME in question.
- A breakdown of the historical financial performance of the SME.
- A comprehensive ratio analysis which incorporates ratios relevant to the credit-making process.
- An overview of the economic positioning of the SME within the current economic cycle.
- An overview of the SME's track record within their industry and an analysis of the major projects which they have completed.
- An analysis of the SME's key clients and suppliers.
- The credit history of the SME.
- An overview as to whether there are any ongoing or completed legal proceedings.
- A comprehensive business valuation which is a major value-add within alternative lending channels.
- Images of the SME's operation, machinery, and capabilities.

The credit ratings measuring overall credibility follow an 8-point scale, which has been compressed from the 20-point scale to better depict the risks associated with SMEs and to remove categories that might not be applicable. The 8-point scale became popular in India when the government launched the Performance and Credit Rating Scheme. Actual SMEs might also find the shortened credit rating scale easier to understand, which is essential as the "AAA-D/20-point" scale can be confusing to non-financial experts (Fig. 3.3).

Apart from the 8-point credit rating scale, some SME rating agencies have adopted slightly shorter scales, such as CariCRIS in the Caribbean, which utilises a five-point scale with seven underlying rating categories. The shorter scale becomes even easier to digest, and Table 3.3 provides an overview of the 5-point rating scale and a description of each of the underlying ratings.

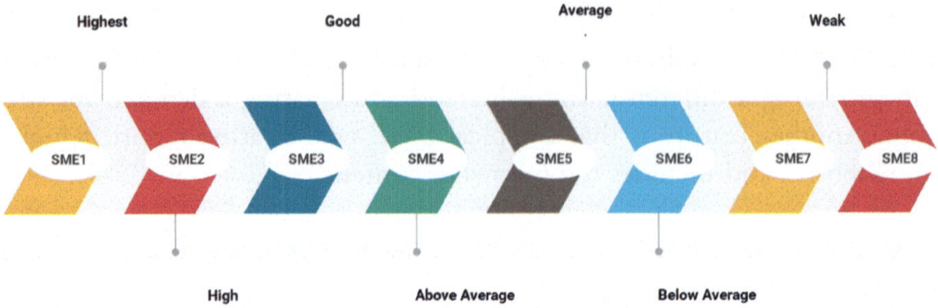

Fig. 3.3 Further insights into the credit quality on a typical 8-point credit rating scale (*Source* SMERA)

Table 3.3 An overview of the 5-point SME credit rating scale

Grade	Definition	Description	Score (%)
SME 1	Excellent	The business showcases excellent business and financial performance	75–100
SME 2 +	Strong	Displays better than average performance with reasonable prospects for improving its performance	70–74
SME 2-	Strong	Displays better than average performance with reasonable prospects for maintaining its performance	65–69
SME 3 +	Good	Displays average performance with reasonable prospects for improving its performance	57–64
SME 3-	Good	Displays average performance with reasonable prospects for maintaining its performance	50–56
SME 4	Below Average	Displays less-than-average performance and below-average prospects for improving or even sustaining its performance	35–49
SME 5	Weak/ Vulnerable	Displays weak performance and is highly vulnerable with low prospects for maintaining viability	0–34

Source CariCRIS (2015)

In comparison to larger firms, SMEs have a tenuous undiversified client base, single revenue streams, limited funding opportunities, and constricted human capital teams. These characteristics limit their ability to be rated highly on a 20-point scale, and the majority are grouped into a few lower bands, making comparability difficult.[17] The rationale behind introducing a

[17] A good example of this in practice can be found within the sovereign rating space, where a large number of emerging market countries are collectively grouped within the single "B" rating category. These countries might differ significantly from a credit quality perspective; however, the rating scale is not designed to depict this explicitly. A specific rating scale could address this issue by better spreading out entities of a similar credit quality across a more well-defined rating scale. This is what effectively occurs within a country rating scale, which is a rating scale running parallel to the standard rating scale but one that is not capped at the sovereign rating. The country scale is mapped to the original rating scale but allows rated entities to be spread out across a broader rating range. For

specific rating scale is to better showcase the relative risks associated with rated entities that have similar characteristics. The 20-point scale, on the other hand, aligns with Basel requirements and better captures the traditional probability of default metrics; the scale is often utilised within bank loan ratings covered below. Lastly, although these ratings are used for access to credit and regulatory purposes, they can also be utilised as an effective due diligence tool. The contents within a standard credit rating report include all of the data that potential clients would be interested in from a due diligence perspective, and the reports can be reconfigured to better serve this purpose. If utilised as a due diligence tool, these ratings can be an effective access to market enabler and could even assist in securing export orders for rated firms. In the next chapter, we discuss two empirical studies that showcase how these ratings can open up market opportunities.

3.4.2 SME Gradings

SME gradings are a type of due diligence product that rates the relative performance of SMEs within a particular sector. These gradings are not intended to capture the probability of default but rather to measure the overall performance of an SME and then compare this to other SMEs within the same sector. This creates a form of ranking within various sectors and provides a platform to showcase the best-performing SMEs.[18] Sector-wide performance averages can be used for comparative purposes and showcase to SMEs their current shortcomings on an industry-wide basis. The grading product can be used across multiple sectors and can even be used as a powerful indirect business development tool. At the beginning of this chapter, we provided insights into how these gradings can be used within the real estate and the educational sector; however, they can also be extended to other key sectors, such as healthcare. Healthcare providers are beginning to operate in an extremely decentralised system whereby services are provided by a combination of large healthcare facilities and smaller medical centres that are set up to cater to specific demographics. Rankings on these smaller medical centres would be a significant value-add to end users as it would provide them with important information that would aid in deciding which medical

example, if a sovereign rating is "B", two hypothetical banks in that country would be capped at a rating of "B" on the standard scale. However, one of them could be rated within the "AAA" category and one at "AA" within a country rating scale (depending on how the rating agencies configure these scales).

[18] Rankings can be provided on an aggregate basis, or they can be provided according to specific metrics or sections within the overall rating methodology.

centres to utilise. This can be an effective tool for countries that want to increase healthcare quality and ensure that it is up to international standards. This could be achieved by configuring the methodologies to international standards and thus providing a benchmark to which healthcare providers can work towards. The grading concept is then a powerful unused concept that can benefit multiple stakeholders and significantly impact both developed and developing countries.

The concept has great potential but is relatively new and would need time to gain popularity. The grading concept was initially popular amongst rating agencies in India; however, the concept has not gained much popularity outside the country. It has recently been utilised within the ESG space in the form of ESG gradings, which are discussed below.

3.4.3 SME Due Diligence Ratings

The SME due diligence concept is born out of the SME credit rating concept and is initiated by entities that want to conduct a third-party review on a related stakeholder. These ratings are similar to SME gradings but exclude the relative performance measurements and have no attached score. Due diligence ratings also differ from traditional credit ratings in that they might exclude some technical financial ratios and include information that would make these reports relevant to their intended audience. As indicated above, SME credit ratings can be used for this purpose; however, the credit rating sections linked to the probability of default and credit rating scales might confuse non-financial end users. The due diligence product solves this by providing ratings that are much more relevant to its intended audience and eliminates complex financial data that might not be appropriate. The due diligence reports, whilst not intended for lending purposes, can be submitted with credit applications to provide borrowers with a better understanding of an SME. This is owing to its ability to decrease the information asymmetry between contracting parties, which is a major hurdle within the access to finance space. There are no limitations to the sectors that are covered, and these due diligence reports can also include a business valuation. Business valuations can be effective when trying to sell a business and can even be used by the purchaser when trying to obtain funding to acquire the same business. These reports can add value when initiating the funding process for alternative investments such as private equity, venture capital, and angel investing. The content within the reports would be relevant to these alternative lenders and can be used as a starting point for a much more in-depth analysis.

The due diligence ratings are also an enabling tool within regional or continental-wide trade areas. The effectiveness of many of these trade areas is often limited by a lack of third-party due diligence reporting, resulting in a reluctance to do business. If due diligence ratings are made widely available, it could significantly enhance trade and provide peace of mind to counterparties within business transactions.

3.4.4 SME ESG Ratings/Gradings

SME ESG ratings and gradings are a fairly new concept that attempts to capture an SME's environmental, social, and governance performance. The grading product measures the performance on a relative basis and provides a benchmark scale that can be used as a reference point for SMEs that want to improve their ESG performance. Due to the nature of SME ESG ratings, they apply to larger SMEs, as measuring micro-enterprises on their ESG performance is challenging and sometimes impractical. The overall ESG rating industry is still in its infancy stage, and the SME ESG industry is a fairly new offshoot from the overall industry. The ESG rating concept, in general, has attracted a great deal of criticism due to a limited amount of standardisation and tenuous levels of regulation. Its development and popularity within the SME space will be highly dependent on the success and adoption of the concept in the traditional ESG rating segment.[19] The overall concept has, however, grown at a rapid pace due to the positive impact that it brings about, and this should continue into the foreseeable future.

There is scope for these ratings in the SME space, but they must be targeted to the correct sectors and be pragmatically applied. For example, these ratings might not apply to micro-enterprises as it is challenging to capture the ESG performance of these organisations. The ratings should then be targeted at larger businesses within the small and medium-sized enterprises category, which could be adequately measured on these metrics.[20] As the overall concept gains in popularity, it will be adopted into the supply chain practices of many large corporates that procure from SMEs; the underlying SME ESG scores could then feed into the ESG scores of these larger companies. In such a scenario, SME ESG ratings will become important, and there will be an increased demand for these ratings. India has recently become one of the first countries to formally regulate these ratings due to the

[19] The traditional ESG segment applies to ESG ratings handed out to large listed and unlisted corporate companies. These companies require these ratings when engaging with other businesses or raising capital, and the ratings have become mandatory for bond issuances in some countries.

[20] This is already being done in some European jurisdictions.

large number of service providers and the widespread use of the concept due to mandatory ESG disclosures.

3.4.5 Bank Loan Ratings

The bank loan rating concept is predominantly available in India and Bangladesh and measures the probability of default within the SME space. The product has been created due to regulatory developments and within the standardised approach for credit assessment, typically in countries that utilise Basel II guidelines. These ratings follow the 20-point rating scale and cover credit exposures within the small and medium enterprise segment. Due to the regulatory nature of these ratings, we do not cover them to a large extent within this publication. The business case for providing these ratings is higher than vanilla credit ratings, and there is a larger market as banks sometimes request that SMEs obtain these ratings prior to obtaining credit facilities. These individual ratings complement banks' overall credit exposure ratings for Basel purposes and add to the accuracy of those ratings due to increased transparency at an individual exposure level.

3.4.6 An Introduction to Backend Credit Scoring Systems

Backend credit scoring systems are offered to banks and financial institutions to complement and boost their internal credit scoring capabilities.[21] These backend systems have been created to increase the limited revenue streams of SME credit rating agencies and leverage their unique credit modelling capabilities. As the section above indicates, SME credit rating agencies have credit rating methodologies for various sectors and sub-sectors. These methodologies are quite valuable to financial institutions as they allow for much more in-depth credit analysis, leading to better credit decisions, increased profitability, and a higher client retention rate.[22] Financial institutions have allocated significant resources to improving their credit scoring capabilities, and SME credit rating agencies have assisted to a large extent with this.

[21] These systems can offer optimised outcomes such as faster credit decisions, improved accuracy, reduced defaults, and satisfied clientele.

[22] These rating agencies are amongst the best at assessing credit risk and have remarkable solutions but struggle to monetise this due to the low profitability levels associated with rating individual SMEs.

SME credit rating agencies, which have struggled with profitability when rating individual SMEs, have negated this by providing these credit scoring systems to financial institutions. The underlying business of rating individual SMEs requires significant scale, which typically takes a long time to build up; simultaneously, providing a backend credit scoring offering allows these SME rating agencies to compensate for the prevalent low-income levels before scale is achieved. Some organisations providing these services do not register as credit rating agencies but rather focus exclusively on providing these services due to the high profitability levels associated with this business model.[23] This is potentially an untapped market for credit rating agencies as a large number of SME credit rating agencies do not provide such services.

3.5 An Introduction to Some of the Ancillary Services which are Linked to the SME Credit Rating Concept

One of the reasons why the SME credit rating concept has not gained much traction is that it is offered in isolation without any other complementary services that can improve its effectiveness. The two prominent ancillary services that come to mind are the SME loan mediation service, which is quite popular in Europe, and the SME rating preparation program, which Credit Rating Analytics has created for a project that the company is busy with.

3.5.1 The SME Loan Mediation Service

The SME loan mediation service is, to some extent, an ancillary service to the SME credit rating concept due to the similarities in their objectives and the manner in which these concepts complement each other. The mediation service has been designed to further enhance access to finance opportunities and undo unfavourable credit decisions handed down to SMEs. These unfavourable credit decisions can either be in the form of SME credit rejections or unfavourable borrowing terms. The SME loan mediation service is generally a government initiative and is quite popular in Europe; it was

[23] A provider of these backend systems is not obligated to register as a credit rating agency and often provides these solutions to credit rating agencies as well.

created in the aftermath of the global financial crisis to alleviate SME funding issues. The mediation service works well in countries with a public sector SME credit rating agency as this gives the mediation unit an in-depth understanding of SME-related credit risk, allowing for effective mediation with financial institutions. Whilst mediating without an SME credit rating agency is possible, it becomes much more effective when including the rating services. Some of the countries with SME credit mediation services or countries that had one are as follows (Table 3.4).

According to OECD statistics, some of these mediation efforts have proven to be highly effective; for example, France's SME loan mediation service has overturned more than 60% of unfavourable credit decisions.[24] Through assisting businesses, the loan mediation service has safeguarded roughly 415,000 jobs and has released €6.8 billion in funding. As per a previous study, around 80% of the mediation services were provided to very small businesses and 70% of the mediation cases were related to:

- Cancellation of financing lines (mainly short-term)
- Refusal of credit.[25]

The mediation service has contributed to France's impressive SME lending statistics but has benefited from the country's large SME credit rating unit. Other factors contributing to the concept's success are that the services are free of charge, the process is quick, it is strictly confidential, and it is available online. The French example highlights the effectiveness of the mediation service and showcases the benefits of combining it with the SME credit rating concept (Fig. 3.4).

We explore the SME loan mediation service in greater detail within Chapter Four.

---

[24] Cusmano, L. (2018). Credit Mediation for SMEs. OECD SME and Entrepreneurship Papers, No. 3, OECD Publishing, Paris, https://doi.org/10.1787/24072c0d-en.

[25] European Foundation for the Improvement of Living and Working Conditions. (2022). Credit mediation structure. [Online]. European Foundation for the Improvement of Living and Working Conditions. https://static.eurofound.europa.eu/covid19db/cases/FR-2008-43_2616.html (Accessed 28 September 2023).

Table 3.4 A list of some of the prominent SME loan mediation providers

Country	Name	Description
Belgium	1819.Brussels[26] And The Corporate Credit Mediator (2009–2011)	Belgium currently has regional mediation services such as those provided by 1819.Brussels. The country previously had a National Corporate Credit Mediator, which was established in 2009 as a component of the "Economic Revival Programme", initiated by the Federal Government and as part of the "Federal Plan for SMEs". The scheme was relatively successful as it managed to unlock €153 million in funding; 60% of cases were successful, and 64% of employment concerned was preserved[27]
Canada	Business Development Bank of Canada (BDC)	The service entails an independent mediation process assisting its clients and the BDC or co-lenders to establish mutually agreeable solutions[28]
Denmark	Danish Banking Association	The Danish Banking Association provides financial mediation and support services to SMEs facing loan-related challenges[29]
France	The SME loan mediation service at Banque de France	Banque de France provides a comprehensive SME loan mediation service that was established in the aftermath of the global financial crisis. The entity is largely successful and managed to change 60% + of unfavourable credit decisions. We discuss this in greater detail below

(continued)

[26] 18.19Hub.Brussels. (2023). Credit Mediator for Brussels Businesses. [Online]. 18.19Hub Brussels. https://1819.brussels/en/information-library/company-financing/credit-mediator-brussels-businesses (Accessed 28 September 2023).

[27] OECD. (2013). Credit Mediation for SMEs. [Online]. OECD. https://www.oecd-ilibrary.org/deliver?redirecturl=http%3A%2F%2Fwww.keepeek.com%2FDigital-Asset-Management%2Foecd%2Fecono (Accessed 28 June 2023).

[28] Business Development Bank of Canada. (2023). Independent mediation process. [Online]. Business Development Bank of Canada. https://www.bdc.ca/en/make-complaint/client/independent-mediation-process (Accessed 20 June 2023).

[29] OECD. (2014). SMEs and the credit crunch: Current financing difficulties, policy measures and. [Online]. OECD. https://www.oecd.org/finance/SMEs-Credit-Crunch-Financing-Difficulties.pdf (Accessed 10 April 2023).

Table 3.4 (continued)

Country	Name	Description
Germany	Various federal and state-level agencies	These agencies provide support and mediation services to SMEs facing financial challenges, including loan-related disputes. The SME loan mediation service ran from– 20092011 and was designed to support SMEs in the aftermath of the global financial crisis[30]
Ireland	The Credit Review Office (CRO) was established in March 2010 under the authority of the Irish Minister for Finance	The CRO functions as an autonomous entity; it includes the Head of the Credit Review Office and a panel of seasoned senior lenders with prior experience in leading financial institutions. The mediation service has proven to be impactful, as it has a success rate in excess of 80%[31]
Malaysia	Financial Mediation Bureau (FMB)	The FMB Offers mediation and financial assistance to SMEs dealing with loan issues[32]
Spain	Spanish Official Credit Institute (ICO)	The ICO provides mediation and financial support to SMEs facing loan-related issues[33]
United Kingdom	The Appeals Process- Launched by the six largest banks in the UK	Although not a formal mediation service by the public sector, the six largest banks in the UK set up the appeals process. Under the appeal process, after a formal request for lending is declined, any business with a group turnover of GBP 25 million or less can make a request for lending, including potential start-ups[34]

[30] OECD. (2013). Credit Mediation fFor SMEs. [Online]. OECD. https://read.oecd-ilibrary.org/economics/credit-mediation-for-smes_24072c0d-en#page2 (Accessed 5 April 2023).

[31] Credit Review. (2023). About Us. [Online]. Credit Review. https://www.creditreview.ie/ (Accessed 5 April 2023).

[32] Fincrew. (2020). Financial Mediation Bureau (FMB). [Online]. Fincrew. https://blog.fincrew.my/2020/11/26/financial-mediation-bureau-fmb/ (Accessed 10 April 2023).

[33] La Moncloa. (2016). ICO Issued 166,000 Loans to Spanish Companies Through its Various Lines for a S. [Online]. La Moncloa. https://www.lamoncloa.gob.es/lang/en/gobierno/news/Paginas/2016/17032016-ico-loans.aspx (Accessed 20 June 2023).

[34] OECD. (2014). Working Party on SMEs and Entrepreneurship (WPSMEE) Credit Mediation for SMEs an. [Online]. OECD. https://www.oecd-ilibrary.org/docserver/24072c0d-en.pdf?expires=1695892204&id=id&accname=guest&checksum=330320E54829053B (Accessed 5 April 2023).

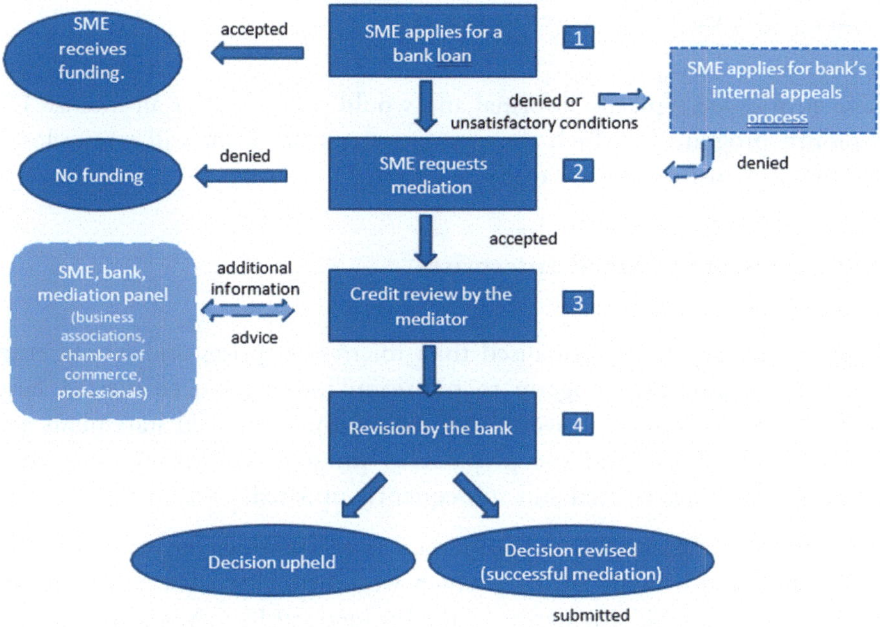

Fig. 3.4 The mediation process (*Source* OECD [2013])

3.5.2 The SME Credit Rating Preparation Program

This concept is not currently available but is one that Credit Rating Analytics created for the project they are assisting an emerging market country with. It is built on the notion that a large portion of the SME population is currently informal, and providing formal ratings to these entities is difficult. These informal SMEs comprise a large portion of the overall SME segment, and excluding them will result in a constricted rating population and limited coverage. To overcome this, the author's firm created the concept of an SME credit rating preparation program, which is specifically designed to better structure SMEs so that they are at the level where they can be rated/graded. The grading preparation program is generally broken up into the following two streams:

3.5.2.1 Stream 1- Micro-enterprises

These entities are typically informal and would need to enter an intense 12–18-month program in which the rating preparation team will work closely with them to ensure they are ready to be rated.

3.5.2.2 Stream 2- Small-enterprises

These entities are more formalised than micro-enterprises and would enter a shorter 6–12-month program to transition into ratable entities. A large number of these businesses would not have formal financial statements and bookkeeping records, and the preparation program will ensure that these financial records are created and subsequently updated.

Furthermore, there could be a preliminary rating product for businesses that are not eligible for credit ratings, which would provide basic due diligence such as approved KYC, the nature of the business, its history, and verification of its owner's claims. Such a product would be a major value-add as this information is generally not available for these businesses; it would also serve as a tangible outcome for entering the grading preparation program.

Some of the services that are included in the grading preparation program are as follows (Table 3.5).

Some nano enterprises might be excluded from the rating process altogether due to the size of their operation and the limited effect that these credit ratings would have on their businesses.[35] The grading preparation program can then be considered an integral component of the overall SME credit rating process and a key enabler to its success. Although the concept has been designed to complement a public sector credit rating agency, it can also be utilised by private sector SME credit rating agencies.

---

[35] This would be in relation to single-owned street vendors, for example, and these businesses might not initially benefit from these ratings in the first place and might be too informal to be considered as being eligible.

Table 3.5 The grading preparation program would include the following activities

Activities included	Further elaboration
Registering the SME and properly structuring it	The first step in the preparation program would be to assist the SME in getting formally registered if there would be merit in doing so. Many SMEs operate as sole proprietors, and an evaluation would need to be done to determine if there would be any benefits to registering as a juristic entity, such as tax efficiencies and other strategic benefits. These entities might be reluctant to formalise themselves because they do not fully understand the potential benefits that can arise. SMEs will also be upskilled on how to best structure their businesses so that considerations such as contingency planning and tax planning are considered
Setting up of business bank accounts	This would be applicable to informal SMEs, which might be operating on a strictly cash basis. A bank account would be the first step in the process of creating a set of financial statements and would be integral to the SME credit rating process. The grading preparation program can work closely with financial institutions that can open up these new accounts on favourable terms
Creating a draft set of financial statements	The preparation program would assist in drafting a set of financial statements, which can be subsequently verified and completed by an accountant. The program can have a database of accountants that SMEs can be referred to. A lack of financial reporting is one of the main inhibiting factors to the SME credit rating process, and resolving this would go far in improving the availability of these ratings

(continued)

Table 3.5 (continued)

Activities included	Further elaboration
Training and capacity-building	This involves training and capacity-building with SMEs on managing a formalised business. It includes concepts such as financial management, compliance-related issues, taxation, and operational management. SMEs will be shown how to better manage and operate their businesses in a formalised structure. This is one of the main value-adds within the preparation program, as SME owners are not very skilled in these subject areas
Upskilling these businesses on risk management as well as contingency and financial planning	Financial and risk planning are key areas within any SME and are heavily linked to lending. SMEs often do not place enough emphasis on this important area, which can inhibit these businesses' ability to access credit facilities. Banks typically require some sort of financial security in the form of collateral or life insurance to ensure that they are covered from a risk management perspective. Many SMEs do not have these financial and risk products in place, and there is a need to upskill these businesses on how to properly structure their financial affairs

References

CariCRIS. (2015). SME Ratings. [Online]. CarisCRIS. https://www.caricris.com/index.php/products-and-services/independent-bond-pricing (Accessed 13 August 2023).

OECD. (2014). Working Party on SMEs and Entrepreneurship (WPSMEE) Credit Mediation for SMEs an. [Online]. OECD. https://www.oecd-ilibrary.org/docserver/24072c0d-en.pdf?expires=1695892204&id=id&accname=guest&checksum=330320E54829053B (Accessed 5 April 2023).

OECD. (2022). Key facts on SME financing. [Online]. Available at: https://www.oecd-ilibrary.org/sites/332ae8cf-en/index.html?itemId=/content/component/332ae8cf-en#:~:text=France-,Key%20facts%20on%20SME%20financing,result%20of%20government%20support%20measures (Accessed 24 March 2023).

SMERA. (2023). SME Credit Rating. [Online]. SMERA. https://www.smeraonline.com/newweb/index.php/sme-rating/ (Accessed 5 December 2023).

4

The Benefits of SME Ratings

Acknowledging and outlining the benefits these ratings can create is important as it showcases the impact of this concept and serves as a motivating factor to introduce it to other countries. As the concept is fairly new, there have not been many concerted attempts to measure the benefits these ratings have managed to bring about. The two prominent studies available include the study completed by the World Bank Group in 2022 and the various studies that the Indian government completed over the duration of the "Credit Rating Performance and Guarantee Scheme". The author's firm completed the study for the World Bank Group, and some of the findings from that primary research effort are a major area of focus in the section below.[1] These findings are also compared to those of the Indian study as the research questions were quite similar, allowing for comparisons. Bespoke impact analysis can be created for countries that want to introduce these ratings in which the economic and socioeconomic benefits are projected.[2]

---

[1] IFC. (2024). The Global Survey of SME Credit Rating Agencies. IFC.

[2] The bespoke impact analysis will measure how the ratings will provide economic and socio-economic benefits to a country, it can be particularly useful when attempting to create a public sector rating agency as it provides context to the upfront costs that will be required to establish a public sector SME rating agency.

S. Pillay, *The Next Frontier in SME Ratings*,
https://doi.org/10.1007/978-3-031-54015-8_4

4.1 An Overview of the Findings from Empirical Studies which have Attempted to Measure the Benefits of these Ratings

It is worth examining this study as it was completed during the course of 2022 and is the most recent independent study that captures the effectiveness of these ratings. The study findings were intriguing as they highlighted the significant benefits these ratings have brought about to rated entities. It focused on rated entities from the following regions: Asia, Africa, and the Caribbean, with the majority of survey responses coming from India, which boasts one of the world's largest private sector SME rating industries. The findings showcased why these ratings should be more widely available as they provided a first-hand account of the impact that they can have on access to credit, access to market, enhancing exporting opportunities, and improving technological improvements within SMEs. The survey participants within the World Bank Group survey were scattered across the following sectors (Fig. 4.1).

As per the infographic above, the majority of survey participants were from the manufacturing sector, with a broad representation from other sectors within the economy.[3] SME credit rating agencies assisted with data collection

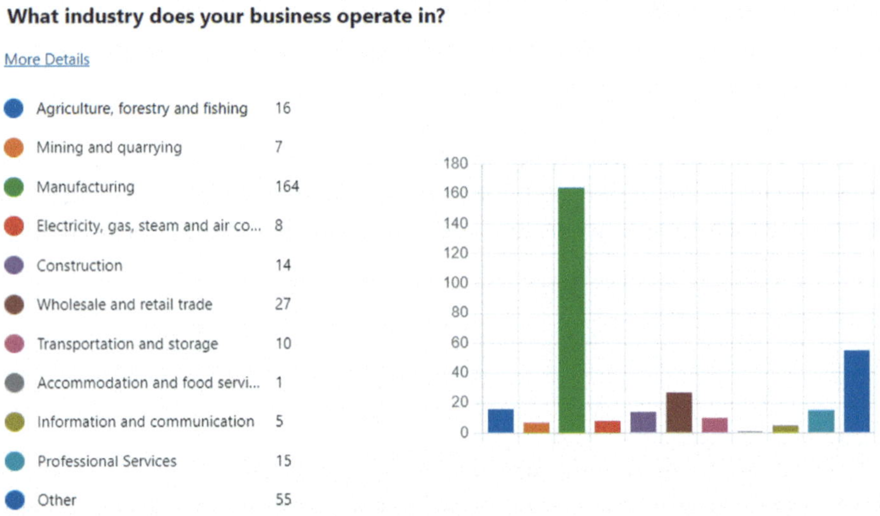

Fig. 4.1 The industry breakdown of survey participants (*Source* IFC [2024])

[3] Within the Indian study, which is quoted in this section, there is also a high representation of SMEs in the manufacturing sector. SMEs were selected randomly in both studies, which indicates

as they sent out these surveys to SMEs that they had rated. The survey population included SMEs from Kenya, India, Bangladesh, and even Trinidad and Tobago. Some of the key findings were as follows:

- *83% of SMEs indicated that these ratings improved their ability to access credit facilities.*

This is arguably the most important finding and highlights how impactful these ratings can be from an access to finance perspective. It also showcases how the information asymmetry between borrowers and lenders plays a major role in inhibiting the ability of SMEs to access credit and how these ratings can mitigate this issue. In most cases, the information asymmetry is the largest within the SME space, and this lack of information, which is not presented in a structured and articulate manner, results in a major disadvantage to SMEs. A large number of SMEs (small or large) do not create comprehensive business reports in a manner that is appealing to financial institutions or related stakeholders. The common approach to presenting such information is to provide financial institutions with financial statements, historical bank statements, and a brief business overview. Furthermore, even if the SME hires a third-party bank intermediary to assist with creating a structured due diligence report, the report will typically not include an independent probability of default or a loss given default calculation. These calculations are informative to financial institutions, and having them readily available assists with the credit-making process. It should also be noted that the rating agencies' ability to measure overall risk using industry-specific methodologies has been a major contributing factor in providing comfort to lending institutions that the inherent risks have been properly calculated. The majority of financial institutions might not have industry-specific rating methodologies, which, if provided by an independent third party, creates additional peace of mind for financial institutions.[4]

Nevertheless, at 83%, the findings within this study imply that the ratings have been effective in achieving their intended mandate of assisting with

that SMEs from the manufacturing sector might have a higher preference to utilise these ratings. It may indicate that they have higher borrowing requirements due to the nature at which these businesses tend to scale up.

[4] Within the project that Credit Rating Analytics completed for the World Bank Group, financial institutions were impressed by these industry-specific methodologies and indicated that this would positively affect their loan-making decisions. These institutions were also intrigued by the depth of the rating reports due to their ability to decrease the information asymmetry between borrowers and lenders significantly.

access to finance. Although much more affirmative, these findings also correlate with the Indian study.[5] The Indian study included a much larger survey population, and there were four studies conducted; some of the findings from the most recent study include: 62% indicated that the NSIC rating helped in securing a loan or credit facilities and 61% of rated entities indicated that the ratings were highly significant for credit approval. The key difference between both studies was that the government-backed study in India included ratings from various rating agencies, and the World Bank study had a large concentration of SMEs that were rated by a single specialist SME rating agency. Nevertheless, the findings are correlated, and both imply that the SME credit rating concept positively impacts access to finance.

- *74% of SMEs indicated that the ratings increased the amount of credit that was extended to them.*

Access to finance is beneficial if the quantum of credit being extended is in line with the borrowing needs of SMEs. The quantum of credit required generally aligns with either short-term needs (generally for liquidity purposes and lower credit amounts) or longer-termed needs (generally for capital expenditure and requiring higher credit amounts). Failure to access funding for capital investment can impede development and result in SMEs falling victim to the SME trap. The SME credit rating concept can alleviate this issue, as evidenced by the 74% of survey participants who indicated that these ratings improved the quantum of credit that was extended to them. The study didn't measure the specific quantum by which credit was increased; however, the findings are still positive. The increase in the quantum of credit is likely due to the decreased information asymmetry between borrowers and lenders and the independent credit opinion. These factors provide comfort to financial institutions as the ratings would allow them to better understand rated entities' financial, operational, technical, strategic, and legal positioning. Due to the difficult initial operating years, many SMEs have previously applied for formal or informal credit facilities and understand the difficulty of obtaining these facilities. The survey responses would then be from an informed perspective and based on their previous engagements with financial institutions.

---

[5] The Indian study measured the outcomes within the "Performance and Credit Rating Scheme for Micro and Small Enterprises", which was initiated by the Indian government. More insights on the study can be found here:

NSIC. (2012). Study of the Performance & Credit Rating Scheme for Micro & Small Enterprises. [Online]. https://www.nsic.co.in/. https://www.nsic.co.in/pdfs/STUDY/srcr2012.pdf (Accessed 3 June 2023).

- *65% of survey participants indicated that these ratings decreased the interest rates charged on credit facilities.*

Gaining access to finance is only beneficial if the interest rate charged is within an affordable range, and this is relevant within the SME space as a large number of SMEs are often charged exorbitant rates. These high interest rates have a major impact on the competitiveness of SMEs and their ability to compete at a local, regional, or even international level. The perceived risks associated with SMEs manifest in the form of exorbitant interest rates, and this is also directly linked to financial institutions not having a clear and concise understanding of the SMEs to which they are extending credit to. This is obviously not the case with all SMEs but is true for a large percentage of SMEs and is often tied to the fact that financial institutions might not deem it feasible to conduct extensive research on an SME, especially if the credit facility being applied for is small. Decreasing the interest rates would naturally be highly beneficial to SMEs, and the survey findings confirmed that SME credit ratings have the ability to do this. This is impressive considering the challenges that SMEs face on this front and is owing to the ratings being able to address the issues presented in the sections above.

- *58% of businesses have reported an increase in the tenure of credit facilities that have been handed out by lending institutions.*

Access to some form of credit is important; however, the underlying tenure is crucial as it is self-destructive to fund long-term projects with short-term funding. This is a result of the liquidity and refinancing issues that occur if credit is provided for short periods or periods that are not aligned with the end use of the borrowed funds. Obtaining short-term credit facilities is quite common within the SME space as financial institutions might not be too confident with the long-term prospects of SMEs due to their existing financial position, technical capabilities, client base, and perceived business survival over the long term. Whilst financial institutions would naturally consider these factors, a key factor overlooked in this scenario is how the tenure of the credit facility would aid in the long-term viability of the business. Financial institutions do not consider this critical aspect but rather focus on how the business would perform based on its existing funding and debt structure. As financial institutions are profit-making entities, having sustainable clients over the long run plays a major role in the long-term viability of their earnings.

- *57% of SMEs indicated that these ratings decreased the amount of collateral that is required to obtain credit facilities.*

One of the major impediments to SMEs' access to finance is their lack of collateral. This is generally very limited within the micro and small business segments. The issue of a lack of collateral is both direct (within the business itself) and indirect (within the business owner's personal capacity). Longer-termed borrowing tenures require collateral to be put forward if the financial institution is not entirely comfortable with the historical and future performance of the SME in question.[6] Furthermore, a lack of access to finance leads to inefficient growth outcomes, hindering SME owners' ability to acquire assets in their personal capacity that could be directly used for collateral in the future, creating a negative feedback loop. The rationale behind the need for collateral is linked to factors covered in the section above; however, a lack of understanding of the SME sector is a major contributing factor, and this is where SME credit ratings can make a major impact. As per the study findings, 57% indicated that the ratings decreased the amount of required collateral. Due to the nature of SMEs and the inherent risk associated with these entities, it would be naïve to suggest that these ratings could eliminate the need for collateral, but a reduction in the quantum of collateral required would improve the ability of SMEs to access credit facilities.

- *70% of SMEs indicated that these ratings improved their accounting record-keeping and the quality and consistency of financial reporting.*

The lack of accounting record-keeping and poor financial reporting are major areas of focus for most governments as they are amongst the key drivers behind SMEs remaining informal.[7] The highly informal nature of these SMEs has knock-on effects on the government's tax collection, their

[6] This figure can be exceptionally high for some countries; for example, within Columbia, 93,3% of SMEs require collateral for borrowing purposes. The phenomenon is not unique to some developing countries as developed countries, such as Switzerland, with strong property laws, had a collateral requirement of 83,9% in 2020. More insights can be found here: OECD. (2022). Financing SMEs and Entrepreneurs 2022: An OECD Scoreboard. [Online]. OECD. https://www.oecd-ilibrary.org/sites/e9073a0f-en/1/3/3/index.html?itemId=/content/publication/e9073a0 (Accessed 14 September 2023).

[7] Within some countries, the number of MSMEs with accounting records is quite low, which excludes many of these businesses from accessing credit. Many SMEs might just keep financial records to measure their performance and avoid drafting financial statements. When looking purely at financial record keeping, the figures are still low; for example, in South Africa, just 46% of micro-enterprises have financial records, and many of these records focus on sales and cash flow data. Such data in isolation will not assist in obtaining credit, and the number of firms with similar data is much lower in the rest of Africa, which creates a significant challenge.

ability to accurately quantify the number of SMEs, and their ability to intervene with critical support initiatives for the SME sector. A lack of accounting record-keeping and measures of financial performance prevents SMEs from incorporating proper financial management measures, which are critical for long-term development. Financial institutions would generally not lend to institutions without any form of financial record-keeping, and this then automatically eliminates a large portion of the overall SME segment as the majority might remain within the informal sector. It is important to note that many SMEs remain short-sighted and do not draft financial statements in an effort to avoid paying taxes. This short-sighted stance keeps them dangerously within reach of the SME trap as it limits their ability to access any form of capital for expansion purposes.[8] This is particularly true for micro and small enterprises, and governments in most jurisdictions have made a concerted effort to address this issue. According to the survey findings, the SME credit rating concept can be viewed as an indirect tool to improve the quality and consistency of accounting record-keeping and financial reporting. At 70%, the improvement is quite substantial as financial record-keeping and reporting are prerequisites to obtaining and maintaining a rating. The ability of SME credit ratings to improve the prospects of securing funding opportunities could entice SMEs to pursue a rating and indirectly formalise these entities. A similar question was put forward in the Indian study, and 58% of survey participants indicated that these ratings had a major impact on the proper maintenance of financial records and audit reports.

- *50% indicated that these ratings improved their ability to secure export orders.*

The number of SMEs that export is low in both developed and developing countries. The major contributing factors to this are a lack of competitiveness, limited due diligence on these entities, and a lack of access to finance. Limited levels of due diligence negatively affect exports as counterparties to a transaction might have concerns about the credibility of the business owner's claims or its ability to complete the order. Many countries in emerging markets have experienced external pressure from a foreign exchange (FX) reserve perspective, and this should intensify given the current economic climate. Achieving an export boost from the SME sector could be highly beneficial to these FX reserves, and the survey findings highlight that these ratings have managed

[8] The SME trap refers to businesses that remain confined to each category of the SME segment or within the overall SME classification. For example, this would refer to small businesses that can't seem to exit out of the small business segment or medium enterprises that can't transition into large businesses.

to assist 50% of survey participants with securing export orders. The primary mechanism behind this is due diligence reporting, which provides extensive information on the exporting firm's capabilities and third-party verification of the business, which provides comfort to the importing firm. Furthermore, the ability of these ratings to improve access to finance results in technological improvements, thus enhancing global competitiveness and the attractiveness of exports. Given the low number of SMEs that currently export, a 50% improvement would be welcomed by most countries and could be a major motivating factor for governments to be willing to introduce the SME rating concept.

Within the Indian study, of the 36% of firms that were exporting, 53% indicated that they benefited from securing additional export orders after getting rated, 42% indicated that the ratings assisted in generating more customer queries, and 57% indicated that it improved customer recognition and acceptability.

- *58% indicated that these ratings assisted with technological improvements within their respective businesses.*

Technological improvements are linked to structural issues such as research and development as well as skill levels within a country. However, as indicated above, it is also strongly linked to the ability of SMEs to access funding opportunities as well as the income-generating capabilities of SMEs. As credit ratings can assist with both access to funding and market access, they could be used as an important tool to enhance technology and improve competitiveness. From the survey responses, 58% indicated that the ratings assisted with technological improvements, which is likely from both a direct and indirect perspective. This is positive and particularly relevant within emerging markets as SMEs in these countries seem to struggle with global competitiveness; many governments have made concerted policy interventions to rectify this, which have had tenuous impacts. Within the Indian study, 50% of survey participants indicated that the ratings assisted with technological improvements in the production process. This corroborates with the World Bank Group project findings and further highlights how these ratings can benefit SMEs.

Some additional key findings from the Indian study which are worth mentioning are as follows:

- 82% of respondents confirmed that financial institutions acknowledged these credit ratings.

- 62% of respondents were willing to renew their credit rating in the next year. This is important as there was no subsidy within the second year, and the rated entity would have to fit the cost for the second-year rating fees.
- 58% of respondents indicated that customers and associates were aware of their company's credit rating.

4.2 The Benefits of these Credit Ratings to Non-Traditional Lending Channels and How these Ratings can be Amended to Complement these Channels

Apart from the directly observable and empirical benefits of these ratings, there can also be deductions made on the potential benefits of these ratings to alternate and non-traditional financing channels. A large majority of the alternative lending channels can benefit from SME credit rating reporting that decreases the information asymmetry associated with SMEs, which at times can be an inhibiting factor to the effectiveness of these lending channels. Within this section, we outline some of the prominent alternative lending channels that are primed to benefit from these ratings. The popularity of these alternative lending channels has increased in recent years as SMEs have become frustrated at the unwillingness of traditional lending channels to extend finance to them on favourable terms. Traditional lending channels are also, at times, guilty of not properly understanding the technical dynamics of new industries and are thus reluctant to extend credit to them. This is particularly true in the tech space, whereby the financial and income generation profiles differ from traditional industries, requiring a different approach to analysing their inherent credibility. Discrepancies such as this have resulted in the exponential growth of the alternate/non-traditional funding channels and some of the prominent channels that can benefit from these ratings can be found in Table 4.1.

An analysis of how SME credit ratings can complement some of the channels mentioned above is as follows:

4.2.1 Asset-based Finance

Asset-based lending and supply chain finance have experienced exponential growth in recent years as they have proven to be effective alternative mechanisms for raising capital. Asset-based finance is where lending takes

Table 4.1 Some of the alternative funding channels which could benefit from SME credit ratings

Asset-based finance	Alternative-debt	Hybrid instruments	Equity instruments
Asset-based lending	Corporate Bonds	Subordinated loans/ Bonds	Private Equity
Factoring	Securitisation Debt	Silent Participations	Venture Capital
Purchase Order Finance	Covered Bonds	Participating Loans	Business Angels
Warehouse Receipts	Private Placements	Profit Participating Rights	Specialised Platforms for Public Listing of SMEs
Leasing	Crowdfunding (debt)	Convertible Bonds	Crowd fundings (Equity)
		Bonds with warrants	
		Mezzanine Finance	

place based on specific assets rather than the overall financial performance of a company. Governments and multilateral organisations have viewed asset-based finance as an untapped funding mechanism, and there have been concerted efforts aimed at increasing the use of this funding channel. One of the key requirements within asset-based finance is transparency, which is sometimes opaque and thus limits the effectiveness of this lending channel. For vanilla asset-based lending channels, SME credit ratings can be useful in that the reports provide a comprehensive overview of the asset base of an SME, including the intrinsic value of these assets, their expected life span, and income-generating capacity. Such information is extremely beneficial as it increases the transparency associated with the underlying assets, thus boosting the prospects of securing funding from this lending channel.

The reverse factoring lending channel has also gained popularity in recent years and is an ever-growing funding channel, with many multilateral organisations placing a major emphasis on it. The concept has, however, received negative publicity in some instances due to scandals such as the Greensill Capital incident.[9] It can be argued that one of the causes behind this scandal was the lack of transparency within the underlying exposures. If SME credit ratings were used to rate the underlying credit exposures, then this would significantly improve transparency and provide a better understanding

[9] Greensill Capital lent money to companies by buying their invoices upfront and collapsed after credit insurers withdrew cover amid concerns over its exposure to the steel and commodity industries. The lack of transparency into the credit quality of the underlying exposures was one of the main downfalls to the business. See Box 5.1.

of the intrinsic credit quality and risks involved.[10] The SME credit rating concept can effectively complement this lending channel, improve investor confidence, and increase its availability within financial markets.

Box 4.1: The Greensill Capital

Greensill Capital was a financial firm which initially focussed on supply chain finance (reverse factoring lending), accounts receivable finance (factoring), and future accounts receivable finance (Smith, 2020). Greensill subsequently ventured into traditional banking via Greensill Bank (Greensill Bank, 2023). All of the supply chain finance activities are based on the underlying procedure of extending credit on the basis of the credit quality/the ability of the counterparty to repay. In the case of Greensill Capital, credit would be extended for such transactions, but there would also be insurance that is taken on the underlying credit quality of these exposures. Greensill Capital had credit agreements with large financial institutions such as Credit Suisse that would provide the capital for them to then on lend within these transactions and insurers such as AIG that would insure their underlying exposures. However, introducing concepts such as future accounts receivable finance, which is based on projected earnings, is an extremely risky value proposition, especially when there is no due diligence done by an independent third party on these exposures. Although Greensill's demise was ultimately owing to extremely risky practices and exposures to a few firms, better oversight of the underlying exposures would have significantly improved the viability of some of these lending transactions. The firm ceased to exist after both the company's financiers (Credit Suisse) and insurers (AIG) pulled the plug.

Purchase order financing has also gained popularity and is an effective mechanism that allows SMEs to access capital based on existing contracts or tenders. In many instances, the major emphasis is placed on the credibility of the counterparty to the underlying contract as they will effectively/indirectly be making the payment. Focus is also placed on the SME applying for the facility, as due diligence will need to be done to determine the ability of the SME to complete the project. SME due diligence, credit ratings, or gradings could assist by comprehensively analysing contracting parties. This will then increase transparency and allow financial institutions to make better-informed decisions. In some instances, SMEs might have sound contracts

[10] Credit Rating Analytics recently contributed to one of the United Nations' main economic development reports in Africa, which unpacked how SME ratings can positively improve the supply chain finance network. More insights can be found here: United Nations Conference on Trade and Development. (2023). Economic Development in Africa Report. [Online]. United Nations. https://unctad.org/system/files/official-document/aldcafrica2023_en.pdf (Accessed 5 August 2023).

in place, but financial institutions might still be weary of the other party's ability to complete the payment on the contract, as well as the SMEs' ability to complete the project. The ratings will ease this process, allowing for much more accurate credit decisions, ultimately resulting in an efficient allocation of capital. The financial institution would also prefer that the ratings originate from a third-party source to eliminate any potential biases that might arise in the event that the counterparties complete the due diligence on themselves.

4.2.2 Alternative Debt

Debt markets for SMEs have developed in recent times, albeit tenuously. This channel allows SMEs to tap into alternative debt pools, which might have a much larger propensity to extend credit to them. Listed SME debt has, for example, allowed fast-growing tech SMEs to tap into an alternative funding source with investors who might have a better understanding of the tech industry than traditional funding sources. The concept has worked well in Europe and has been complemented by the availability of SME credit ratings. Whilst SME credit ratings are not a prerequisite for delving into the listed debt market, these ratings have proven to be quite effective at reducing the information asymmetry that exists on these exchanges. This has major benefits to this funding channel as it can decrease borrowing costs for SMEs and simultaneously increase investor appetite for such issuances. A recent study by the European Central Bank showcased that SMEs that tapped into alternative debt markets had received lower bank borrowing costs for similar maturities; this was on a relative basis to non-issuing SMEs.[11] This then showcases the importance of diversifying funding sources and the impact that it can have on the lending monopoly that traditional banks enjoy within the SME space. As discussed in other chapters of this book, the information asymmetry that exists within the SME space is significant, and a greater asymmetry may exist within the alternative debt space. Within the listed debt space, in particular, the ratings can also be provided on a shadow basis and initiated by the exchanges which provide the platform for these listings. Doing this increases the appetite of potential investors who might not be satisfied with just bond prospectuses, increasing the use of these exchanges. However, debt markets for SMEs require strong property laws, which are sometimes

[11] Ongena et al. (2020). Bank Credit and Market-based Finance for Corporations: The Effects of Minibond i. [Online]. ECB Working Paper Series. https://www.ecb.europa.eu/pub/pdf/scpwps/ecb.wp2508~784b4b2237.en.pdf (Accessed 5 September 2023).

unavailable in many emerging market countries. The unlisted debt market is negatively affected to a larger extent when these laws are not available, as they are associated with significant information asymmetries. SME credit ratings could serve as an effective tool within the unlisted debt space and promote its appeal to potential investors.[12]

The listed SME equity space has proven to be an effective concept in theory; however, practical applications have provided mixed results, with many of these SME exchanges not achieving their intended objectives. A large number of developing and developed countries have set up SME equity exchanges as a tool for larger SMEs to tap into alternative funding pools. A significant number of these equity exchanges have proven to be unsuccessful due to limited or low levels of liquidity. Low levels of liquidity have been one of the major shortcomings which have decreased the appeal for listing or trading in these securities. Analyst coverage is one of the reasons behind the low levels of liquidity, which results in investors not having sufficient information to make informed investment decisions. The costs of analyst coverage on both the buying and selling side are high, and the profitability associated with these securities does not make financial sense to investment banks (sell-side) or asset management firms (buy-side). SME credit ratings can, however, be used as an alternative form of analyst coverage and a much more cost-effective solution. The SME due diligence product, in particular, can be slightly reconfigured and used as an effective tool providing comprehensive coverage of SMEs' financial, operational, compliance, and strategic performance. This coverage could be useful to potential investors who might be interested in these securities but are reluctant due to limited data availability. The due diligence ratings could also be used as a tool to initiate the research process and as the starting point for further research. When used for this purpose, the ratings are not purely limited to listed equity but can be used in unlisted equity and hybrid transactions. Data availability within the unlisted equity space remains constricted, and any improvements to this could play a major role in increasing the use of this funding channel.

[12] Investors in unlisted debt might naturally be sceptical if there is no credible third-party due diligence, as weak property laws would decrease the probability of recouping parts of their investment if a default occurs.

4.3 SME Credit Ratings and a Post-COVID-19 Environment

The COVID-19 pandemic has been devastating to all stakeholders and showcased how exogenous shocks can wreak havoc on the most established and well-diversified businesses. The negative effects of the pandemic will result in many SMEs not returning to business, a reluctance by individuals to take up the entrepreneurship route, and tarnished financial records of businesses and their respective owners. The digital economy that the COVID-19 pandemic has ignited has also changed the SME landscape and the way in which business is being carried out.[13] These newly formed digital business segments are sometimes non-traditional, resulting in financial institutions not having a firm grasp on how to evaluate them, making things difficult from a funding perspective. SME credit ratings within this environment can play a major role in expediting the sector's recovery and alleviating some of the shortcomings mentioned in the section above. These ratings' ability to open up funding and market opportunities could be extremely beneficial and would complement many of the existing interventions by key stakeholders. It can also be argued that SME credit ratings could have played a role in accentuating response mechanisms to the pandemic, which were often ineffective in achieving their intended mandates. For example, many of the guarantee schemes that governments initiated were ineffective in that financial institutions were still reluctant to extend credit to the private sector.[14] If SME credit ratings were used to complement these guarantee schemes, it could have resulted in a larger quantum of credit being extended as the ratings would address the information asymmetry, which was one of the largest impeding factors. The ability of these ratings to facilitate access to alternative funding channels could have also been a major advantage during the pandemic, as these channels might have had a larger funding appetite. If an SME was in the business of providing PPE equipment at the onset of the COVID-19 pandemic and their historic turnover was not significant, traditional credit applications would not have factored in potential business opportunities and would have been retrospective in nature. These businesses might not have obtained the requisite funding to expand within the onset of the pandemic,

[13] Although the pandemic has had predominantly negative effects, there have been some positives, as a handful of the digital channels have highlighted how efficiencies can be gained by transferring to these channels.

[14] This phenomenon was experienced in both developed and developing economies and provided false hopes to many SMEs upon the announcement of these interventions.

which could have been lucrative from a business perspective. The forward-looking nature of SME credit ratings may have assisted as it would have assessed the SMEs' positioning in the economic cycle. Incorporating such an analysis thus increases the appetite of financial institutions to provide funding to these businesses.

SME ratings can then be used as a vital tool to prop up the SME sector in a post-COVID-19 environment. This will, however, depend on the availability of these ratings, and the subsequent chapters of this book are dedicated to how the concept can be introduced into both developing and developed economies.

4.4 Utilising these Ratings for Micro-enterprises

Although the SME rating concept focuses on SMEs and excludes micro-enterprises in some jurisdictions, the concept can also be extended to these smaller entities. However, the value proposition needs to be adjusted to better depict the risks associated with this segment, which is a value-add to related stakeholders.[15] The primary reason behind excluding micro-enterprises is the difficulty of rating these entities due to their informal nature. Many of these entities might not meet the core requirements to be eligible for ratings, such as being registered, having a registered bank account, or having basic financial statements. To address this issue, rating agencies could take an out-of-the-box approach by designing a rating preparation program to bring these entities up to the level where they are eligible for these ratings. The previous chapter provided an overview of the rating preparation program, and Chapter Seven provides some insights into how the concept is being introduced within the country that Credit Rating Analytics is currently working with.

Micro-enterprise ratings might be clustered within a similar rating band due to the homogenous nature of the financial viability of these entities. For example, a larger number of these entities might have a limited number of larger customers, little or no diversification in their revenue streams, unfavourable payment terms with creditors, limited or no credit facilities, an

[15] Adjusting the value proposition will also entail changes to the rating process to make it viable for both SMEs as well as the rating agencies providing these valuable services. It is important to note that the fee income would be reduced even further as micro-enterprises would have a lower propensity to pay for these services, and the service offering would then need to change to account for this.

unskilled labour force, or the entire operation being spearheaded by one individual and heavily correlates with the business/economic cycle. The ratings collectively will then be clustered within similar rating bands, requiring bespoke rating scales that could better showcase the inherent credit quality and be more useful to end users. The traditional 20-point rating scale might not be ideally suited, and a shorter rating scale would be better for showcasing credit quality differentiation within this segment. This approach was taken within India's performance and credit rating scheme, in which an 8-point credit rating scale was established. The 8-point rating scale is similar to a country rating scale, which was created to better depict credit risk within an underlying country that might be capped by a sovereign rating.[16] The 8-point rating scale would then enhance the effectiveness of these ratings with end users, better depict the risks associated with these entities, and increase comparability.

To ensure the maximum benefit of these ratings and to boost economic output, it is imperative that micro-enterprises are included, as they generally make up the largest number of enterprises within most countries. The only issue that arises is profitability within this segment due to the cost-conscious nature of these entities. A compelling value proposition and business model is required to ensure that it makes financial sense, and we touch on this in the next section. One of the major drawbacks of the SME credit rating industry is the fixation with replicating the credit rating process associated with rating large companies. Taking this approach has resulted in unfavourable outcomes for rating agencies and SMEs, highlighting the need for a different approach. The entire value proposition needs to be repositioned so that the rating process is streamlined and the service offering is better aligned with the needs of SMEs.

[16] If a sovereign is rated "B" for example, the majority of underlying ratings within the country would be capped under the "B" category. Introducing a country scale can then expand the B category to a full rating scale which would include "AAA" all the way to "D", although the ratings are technically capped at "B" outside of the country rating scale, the 20-point country scale would allow for better differentiation of credit quality amongst rated entities.

References

Greensill Bank. (2023). Home: Greensill Bank. [Online]. Greensill Bank. https://www.greensill-bank.com/ (Accessed 14 September 2023).
IFC. (2024). The Global Survey Of SME Credit Rating Agencies. IFC.
Smith, R. (2020). Greensill and Supply-chain Finance: How a Contentious Funding Tool Works. [Online]. Financial Times. https://www.ft.com/content/1bbbe94c-9c3d-43d1-bcdd-8add6557c5a7 (Accessed 14 September 2023).

Part III

The Public Sector SME Credit Rating Model

This section unpacks the public sector credit rating model and how it can be incorporated within the SME credit rating industry. We explore how the public sector model has worked in countries that have utilised the concept and provide recommendations on how it could be introduced in other countries. It should be noted that the public sector credit rating model has garnered a great deal of attention in the aftermath of the global financial crisis, with many practitioners and stakeholders calling for its adoption as an alternative to the private sector credit rating industry. Whilst most of these attempts have not amounted to much, the public sector SME credit rating model has flourished in Europe and positively impacted access to finance within this crucial sector. The concluding chapters of this section outline how the public sector SME credit rating model can be brought to fruition. The author's consulting firm (Credit Rating Analytics) is currently working as a lead advisor to an emerging market country to create the world's largest SME grading agency (public or private).[1] The proposed grading agency in question significantly focuses on access to market and credit; some of the insights gained from that project are outlined in this section.

[1] Within this project, we use the term grading and not rating as it has a larger focus on access to market, which is synonymous with the grading concept. These gradings can, however, be used for access to credit, as discussed in Chapter Three above.

5

An Introduction to the Public Sector Model

5.1 The History Behind the Public Sector Credit Rating Model and the Attempts to Create a Public Sector Credit Rating Agency

The public sector credit rating model related to traditional credit ratings has gained significant levels of interest in the aftermath of the global financial crisis, with many attempts being made to establish a public sector alternative to the private sector industry.[1] The rationale behind such attempts is due to deficiencies with the private sector model, which has been viewed as a key contributing factor to the global financial crisis. Many academics and stakeholders with a vested interest in financial markets, capital allocation, or the credit rating industry have discussed the prospects of a public sector/non-profit credit rating agency as an alternative to the private sector model. Some of the pertinent factors behind calls for the creation of a public sector or non-profit model are discussed Table 5.1.

The shortcomings above have resulted in concerted efforts to find an alternative to the credit rating industry in its current form. Initial recommendations revolved around credit rating reform, which was enacted as

[1] It is well reported that credit rating agencies played an implicit role in the global financial crisis by providing inaccurate or profit-driven credit opinions on mortgage-backed and related securities. These ratings drove investment decisions, resulting in investments into extremely risky securities, which were rated quite highly by the credit rating agencies; some instruments were given the highest ratings ("AAA") just days before going bankrupt.

S. Pillay, *The Next Frontier in SME Ratings*,
https://doi.org/10.1007/978-3-031-54015-8_5

Table 5.1 The rationale behind interest in the public sector model

Shortcomings of the Private Sector Model	Further elaboration
The conflicts of interest with the issuer pays model	The issuer pays model is flawed with potential conflicts of interest due to rated entities paying for their own credit ratings. The underlying financial incentive can sometimes result in inflated or false credit ratings being handed out. Evidence of the conflicts of interest associated with this model could be seen within the global financial crisis (GFC), in which many inflated credit ratings that didn't reflect the underlying intrinsic value of rated entities/ securities were issued. End users of these ratings (investors) face the negative blowout from these incorrect credit assessments, and this has been the basis for major industry reforms in the aftermath of the global financial crisis. One of the primary drivers behind the public sector model is to provide an alternative to the profit-maximising nature of private-sector credit rating agencies. The public sector model is viewed as an alternative that might take a different approach due to its operating model and mandate
	The alternative to the issuer-pays model is the investor-pays model, which was previously the predominant model used. The model might have greater foresight and is associated with having a lower proclivity to issue false credit ratings due to its detached link with the rated entity.[2] The model is not exempt from conflicts of interest as there have been instances where favourable ratings were handed out to securities widely held by subscribers of the rating agency utilising the investor-pays model. However, the frequency of such conflicts of interest is much lower than in the issuer pays model[3]
A lack of legal or regulatory penalties is associated with the private sector model	Academics, civil society, and related stakeholders have often questioned the lack of regulatory penalties or legal action against the credit rating industry. Whilst credit rating agencies have incurred regulatory penalties in the aftermath of the global financial crisis, many critics of the industry have indicated that these penalties have been tenuous and failed to prevent further conflicts of interest from arising. However, the frequency of these credit rating penalties has increased over the past few years, and Annexure One summarises some of the pertinent instances in which credit rating agencies were fined. Some countries might also not have the requisite regulatory frameworks in place, which can result in questionable behaviour on the part of the credit rating agencies[4]

(continued)

[2] Egan Jones was the first to downgrade both World Com and Enron and predicted/warned of the global financial crisis of 2008: Egan Jones (2023). Company overview. [Online]. Egan Jones. https://www.egan-jones.com/about-us/company-overview/ (Accessed 14 September 2023).

[3] Bonsall et al. (2018). Conflicts of interest in subscriber-paid credit ratings. [Online]. *Journal of Business Ethics*, Forthcoming. https://papers.ssrn.com/sol3/papers.cfm?abstract_id=3270894# (Accessed 14 September 2023).

[4] There have, however, been many improvements on this front as many countries have introduced some form of regulation, either in the form of comprehensive regulatory frameworks or registration requirements. These interventions have increased the oversight of credit rating agencies but have not eliminated the conflicts of interest associated with this sector.

Table 5.1 (continued)

Shortcomings of the Private Sector Model	Further elaboration
A lack of consistency in the manner in which credit ratings are handed out	Issuers and related commentators in developing economies have often questioned the consistency in which credit ratings are handed out within developed versus developing economies. Perceived discrepancies in this regard have then created doubt in the authenticity of the credit rating industry by stakeholders who might feel unfairly treated. Multiple stakeholders have raised this issue, and it is one of the primary drivers behind initiatives to create regional or continental-wide credit rating agencies. As per the examples provided below, a large number of these efforts have been in the sovereign rating space, as this is where the largest number of perceived inconsistencies exist
The high levels of profitability within the traditional credit rating business result in a limited focus on other important sectors or segments within the credit rating industry	This can be viewed as a major shortcoming and is heavily linked to the SME credit rating concept put forward within this book. The traditional credit rating industry is highly profitable, resulting in existing rating agencies focusing exclusively on the business segments associated with the traditional industry (corporate, financial institutions, sub-sovereign, derivative, and project-based ratings).[5] These segments offer high profit margins and require modest levels of scale to ensure profitability. The rating agencies then stay clear of other segments, such as the SME space, which only offers profitability if significant scale is achieved. Multinational organisations have attempted to increase the quantum of traditional rating agencies that focus on the SME sector due to the broader benefits that it would bring about. As pointed out in other chapters, the SME rating concept has proven to be highly effective, resulting in some governments deciding to take the public sector approach to roll out these ratings
Credit rating agencies are unwilling to enter countries with low levels of profitability	This is in reference to the overall credit rating industry and the reluctance of credit rating agencies to provide coverage to a large number of countries within developing countries. For example, around 38% of countries in Africa have no sovereign credit rating coverage from the big three rating agencies, which negatively affects the potential funding opportunities of entities in these countries.[6] Having no sovereign ratings also has major negative effects on financial sector development and overall economic development. Although credit ratings have received negative publicity in the aftermath of the global financial crisis, the concept plays an integral part in the functioning of the overall financial system, and their exclusion can cause financial systems to develop at a much slower pace. Apart from this, they tend to increase funding opportunities for the private and public sectors, thereby boosting economic development. For example, within most unrated countries, governments borrow heavily from banks as this is one of the only financing options; the public sector is also viewed as the most credible client due to its unique ability to monetize debt. The introduction of credit ratings in these countries opens up funding opportunities

(continued)

[5] Profitability levels within the traditional credit rating industry exceed 40% in many instances, which is high on a relative basis to most industries. This then makes it extremely tempting to re-invest profits into growing these businesses as it exceeds the opportunity costs of deploying capital elsewhere.

[6] This low level of coverage has been one of the deciding factors which has resulted in the African Union wanting to establish an African credit rating agency.

Table 5.1 (continued)

Shortcomings of the Private Sector Model	Further elaboration
	for governments as capital market options become available; this frees up capital within the banking sector, allowing for increased borrowing from the private sector.[7] However, as these are profit-maximising entities, it is of no fault of their own to operate in this manner as they have no obligation to enter unprofitable markets. This approach has resulted in affected stakeholders wanting to take different approaches and look into concepts such as the public sector rating model, which can be used as a viable tool to provide coverage to jurisdictions that traditional rating agencies might have no appetite for

either an update to credit rating regulation or the creation of regulations in markets where there were none. However, there were also alternate suggestions, such as the creation of public sector rating agencies in which the state or multilateral organisations took the lead and handed out credit ratings as a viable alternative to the private sector industry. Academics and key financial industry stakeholders put forward the creation of such public sector credit rating agencies. Some of the efforts to do so can be found in Table 5.2.

As evidenced above, various stakeholders have made a few attempts to look into alternatives to the traditional credit rating industry, with the public sector model being touted as a potential alternative. The pertinent reasons which arise related to why these public sector rating agencies have not come to fruition boil down to the legal implications of inaccurate ratings, the financial implications of creating an organisation of such scale, the demand for these ratings, and the perceived impact that the ratings will provide. The impact is a major factor as it is not feasible to make such a large outlay to establish a public sector rating agency if the rating agency is not going to make an impact on financial markets. A study was conducted when there was talk of an EU-controlled rating agency, which found that ratings outside of the big two have little impact on bond yields. It was then determined that if a public sector rating agency entered the market, the rating agency would have no effect as there would be additional concerns related to the credibility of the ratings handed out.[8]

The public sector SME rating model, which focuses exclusively on rating small and medium enterprises via a public sector credit rating agency, has

[7] Luitel, P., & Vanpee, R. (2018). How Do Sovereign Credit Ratings Help to Financially Develop Low-Developed Countries? https://papers.ssrn.com/sol3/papers.cfm?abstract_id=3287881 (Last accessed 2 September 2023).

[8] Altdörfer et al. (2019). The Case for a European Rating Agency: Evidence from the Eurozone Sovereign Debt. [Online]. *Journal of International Financial Markets, Institutions and Markets*. https://www.sciencedirect.com/science/article/abs/pii/S1042443118301847 (Accessed 15 July 2023).

Table 5.2 Previous attempts at creating an alternative credit rating model

Attempts to create an alternative to the existing credit rating industry	Further insights into these attempts and the eventual outcome
1. The credit research initiative at the National University of Singapore	The Credit Research Initiative (CRI) is a non-profit undertaking at the National University of Singapore committed to advancing big data analytics and providing directly useful credit intelligence to the professional and academic communities.[9] Due to its non-profit nature, it can be viewed as an alternative model to the existing credit rating industry. Its credit assessments utilise the latest technologies and follow a slightly different approach to the traditional industry. The concept is, however, still in its infancy stage, and there is not widespread global coverage at this point
2. Prominent leaders from the European Union, such as Angela Merkel, called for the establishment of a public sector credit rating agency in 2010[10]	The call for establishing such an organisation gained momentum in 2011 when the European Parliament called for an impact analysis on establishing an independent European Credit Rating Foundation. Upon completion, the impact analysis determined that the rating agency would add little value and that it could bring about unwarranted legal implications. The call for the public sector model was on the backdrop of the European sovereign debt crisis in which many European countries were downgraded due to perceived deterioration in their underlying credit quality. The idea has not gained any momentum since, and there have been no further calls to look into the concept
3. A proposal by consultancy firm Roland Berger (Germany) in 2011, to create a public sector rating agency[11]	The consultancy firm proposed a public sector rating agency that would be an alternative to the private sector credit rating industry. This was done in 2011, and the concept was subsequently pursued by other organisations, such as the Bertelsmann Foundation, as outlined below

(continued)

[9] National University of Singapore: Credit Research Initiative. (2023). THE CRI AT A GLANCE. [Online]. National University of Singapore: Credit Research Initiative. https://nuscri.org/en/about/ (Accessed 14 September 2023).

[10] EUobserver. (2010). Merkel Backs Creation of European Credit Rating Agency. [Online]. EUobserver. https://euobserver.com/green-economy/30001 (Accessed 14 September 2023).

[11] Mckay, Z. (2012). Roland Berger: Rating Europe. [Online]. Forbes. https://www.forbes.com/sites/insead/2012/07/06/roland-berger-rating-europe/?sh=665a45a7167c (Accessed 14 August 2023).

Table 5.2 (continued)

Attempts to create an alternative to the existing credit rating industry	Further insights into these attempts and the eventual outcome
4. The Bertelsmann Foundation in 2012 attempted to create a non-profit credit rating agency	This was an effort by the Bertelsmann Foundation to create a non-profit credit rating agency focusing on sovereign ratings. The rating agency was referred to as The International Non-Profit Credit Rating Agency (INCRA) and was to be funded by governments, private donors, multilateral organisations, and related stakeholders.[12] The project received an abundance of attention during its initial years but never came to fruition as it had a high establishing cost of $400,000,000, and it was difficult to get a buy-in from various stakeholders. Pilot ratings were handed out via the proposed rating agency, but these efforts were still insufficient to get the concept off the ground[13]
5. An attempt by the BRICS nations in 2017 to create a public sector rating agency within the BRICS region	The BRICS group of nations was keen on establishing a public sector regional rating agency covering rated entities within the BRICS region. The proposed enterprise did gain sufficient traction, and a feasibility study was completed to determine whether the organisation should be set up The concept was also brought before the BRICS business council, which decided that instead of creating a public sector rating agency, there should rather be a credit rating alliance between rating agencies within the BRICS region.[14] These findings and some of the recommendations from the feasibility study resulted in the organisation not being established. There are still discussions around the prospects of setting up this entity; however, there have not been additional efforts to look into the concept. This might change with the discussion of a BRICS-backed common currency as there could be synergies between the credit rating agency and the common currency
6. An ongoing attempt by the African Union to create a public sector ACRA (African credit rating agency)	The request to look into the prospects of creating an AU-controlled credit rating agency was put forward during the African Union's 3rd Specialised Technical Committee Meeting on Finance, Monetary Affairs, Economic Planning, and Integration in March 2019. The United Nations Economic Commission for Africa partially funded the project, and the African Union selected Credit Rating Analytics to complete the initial feasibility study. The key findings were presented in 2021; however, there are still ongoing attempts at bringing this organisation to fruition

[12] Annette Heuser. (2014). An Update on My Non-profit Credit Rating Agency, which could Revolutionise how Economies are Graded. [Online]. Ted Blog. Available at: https://blog.ted.com/an-update-on-my-non-profit-credit-rating-agency_/ (Accessed 10 September 2023).

[13] INCRA. (2012). Country Ratings Report. [Online]. bertelsmann-stiftung. https://www.bertelsmann-stiftung.de/fileadmin/files/BSt/Presse/imported/downloads/xcms_bst_dms_36967 (Accessed 10 August 2023).

[14] BRICS Business Council. (2023). Annual Report 2022/2023. [Online]. BRICS Business Council. https://brics2023.gov.za/wp-content/uploads/2023/08/SABBC-AR-30-Aug.pdf (Accessed 15 July 2023).

evolved out of the idea phase into a fully-fledged organisation providing a vital service to SMEs in Europe. This is the only known form of a public sector credit rating system and has proven to be largely effective. One of the reasons for its success is that it is not plagued by shortcomings that prevented the above-mentioned organisations from being established. There are currently seven public sector SME rating agencies which are housed as units within central banks in Europe; these are:

1. The SME credit rating unit at Banco de Espana (BBK);
2. The SME credit rating unit at Banque de France (BdF);
3. The SME credit rating unit at Banca d'Italia (BdI);
4. The SME credit rating unit at Banco de Portugal (BdP);
5. The SME credit rating unit at Banka Slovenjie (BS);
6. The SME credit rating unit at Deutsche Bundesbank (BBk) and
7. The SME credit rating unit at Oesterreichische Nationalbank (OeNB)[15]

These central banks have created these SME credit rating units to serve as In-house Credit Assessment Systems (ICAS), and none of them are registered with the European Securities and Market Authority due to their operating and ownership models. Banque de France officially applied for an exemption from ESMA, which was granted and published in the Official Journal of the European Union on June 19, 2010.[16] These ICAS are, however, directly monitored by national risk management functions and the ECB's Directorate of Risk Management. The SME credit rating unit at Banque de France (BdF) is the largest SME rating agency in the world, and it is on both an absolute and per capita basis.[17] The organisation demonstrates that the public sector has the required scale to provide these services on a country-wide basis and simultaneously deliver a sophisticated value proposition. It is important to note that the ratings provided by these central banks are held in high regard; for example, BDF's SME ratings are not only utilised for traditional lending at a firm level but are also trusted within very complex derivative issuances

[15] Banco de España Eurosistema. (2021). Overview of Central Banks' in-house Credit Assessment Systems in the Euro Area. [Online]. Banco de España Eurosistema. https://www.bde.es/f/webbde/SES/Secciones/Publicaciones/PublicacionesSeriadas/DocumentosOcasionales/21/Files/do2131e.pdf (Accessed 21 March 2022).

[16] Rating platform. (2023). Banque de France FIBEN. [Online]. Rating Platform. https://www.ratingplatform.com/agency_view.php?id=45 (Accessed 5 March 2022).

[17] Banque de France's credit rating unit is also larger than any individual private sector credit rating agency, and this is by a large margin as well. The largest private sector credit rating agencies can be found in India but the number of ratings handed out by these entities is much lower.

such as SME structured note issuances and within minibond listings.[18] The effectiveness of these ratings, the scale at which they are handed out and the investor trust are clear evidence of the effectiveness of the public sector model. These SME credit rating units also complement other central bank activities, such as their in-house SME loan mediation services. Banque de France, for example, has an SME loan mediation service created in the aftermath of the global financial crisis to assist SMEs with access to finance. The mediation service has proven to overturn unfavourable credit decisions in more than 60% of cases which are linked to both credit rejections and unfavourable borrowing terms. The SME credit rating unit would naturally complement the mediation service well as it provides an in-depth understanding of businesses that BdF simultaneously rates. The SME loan mediation offering as an ancillary service is discussed within the subsequent chapters, where we unpack how a public sector SME rating agency can be established.

Outside of Europe, the public sector SME credit rating model has not managed to gain much traction, with no similar organisations providing these services. The closest to this would be the internal SME credit rating units at multilateral development organisations, which provide these ratings exclusively to projects linked to these organisations. For example, the SME credit rating units at both the Khalifa Fund in Abu Dhabi and the Dubai Chamber provide a comprehensive SME credit rating offering to SMEs or projects funded by these organisations. Many development organisations in other jurisdictions provide a similar offering; however, there have been few attempts at creating a public sector country-wide SME credit rating agency. The primary reason behind this is a lack of awareness of both the SME credit rating concept and the public sector model through which this can be rolled out. Officials are also put off by some of the shortcomings which have prevented public sector rating agencies that focus on traditional credit ratings from coming to fruition, some of which were discussed above. One of the reasons behind writing this book is to increase the awareness of this concept, which can hopefully culminate in increased availability of these ratings via either the public or private sector models. The project that Credit Rating Analytics is working on with an emerging market government will be a great case study on the viability of creating such an entity outside of Europe, which can be used as a benchmark for other countries wanting to do something similar.

[18] Minibonds are listed fixed-income issuances by SMEs, which allow these SMEs to raise capital directly from stock exchanges in Europe. These issuances do not require SME credit ratings; however, the ratings complement these issuances well by decreasing the information asymmetry, which can potentially lead to lower borrowing costs.

5.2 The Rationale Why a Public Sector SME Credit Rating Agency could be a Viable Solution

In contrast to the shortcomings of the public sector credit rating agency model focusing on traditional credit ratings (all of which have failed to come to fruition), the structure, risks, and effectiveness of the public sector SME credit rating model make it a viable solution. This is primarily owing to:

1. The types of ratings handed out and the inherent risks,
2. The demand for these ratings,
3. The lack of appetite from the private sector to enter this market and,
4. The willingness of the public sector to uplift the SME sector.

The author's own view is that there is merit in considering the public sector as a viable option as the underlying concept is not very profitable, and the private sector is thus reluctant to roll out these important services on a broad-scale basis.[19] The industry structure indicates that traditional credit rating agencies (focusing on sovereign, corporate, and derivative ratings) venture into the SME credit rating space. These traditional rating agencies are generally exposed to significant profit margins within their core business, making them reluctant to invest heavily in the less profitable SME credit rating space. The SME credit rating industry requires scale to make it profitable, and this, in turn, requires significant investment in operational capacity, which a few rating agencies are willing to do. Whilst the private sector can provide a remarkable and impactful service to SMEs, the important question is whether they are willing to make the requisite investment to have these services readily available on a broad-scale basis. In order to achieve such scale, additional intervention is needed, possibly in the form of government grants similar to those provided in India. Additional insights on India's government-backed scheme can be found in Box 5.1.

[19] A large number of SME credit rating agencies or SME credit rating units within established rating agencies are either operating with breakeven or unprofitable margins. This is specifically related to rating individual SMEs and does not include other services such as backend credit scoring systems.

Box 5.1: The Performance and Credit Rating Scheme for Micro & Small Enterprises

The Performance and Credit Rating Scheme for Micro & Small Enterprises was a public/private sector initiative which included key stakeholders such as the Ministry of MSME, the Indian Banks' Association (IBA), the Central Bank, and Credit Rating Agencies (Ministry of Micro, Small & Medium Enterprises, 2015). The scheme was launched in April 2005 and provided a subsidy to SMEs to obtain SME ratings. The subsidy was up to 75% of the rating fee in year one, and SMEs were rated on an 8-point rating scale. MSMEs within the scheme could select the rating agency that they wanted to obtain a rating from and were responsible for the second year's surveillance fees. Within this ecosystem model, SMEs could obtain preferential borrowing rates if they were highly rated, and the scheme proved to be quite effective at improving access to finance as well as access to market opportunities. One of the scheme's objectives was to provide an independent third-party assessment of an SME, which could showcase their strengths and weaknesses. Identifying the weaknesses was an important feedback mechanism to allow SMEs to understand their shortcomings and boost long-term growth and development. The multistakeholder approach proved to be quite effective, and various studies have showcased that the ratings were very effective in improving access to finance metrics, access to market metrics and improvements to the formalisation of SMEs via enhancements to financial reporting and accounting record-keeping. The government conducted various studies over the period, and some of the tangible benefits are quoted in the sections below. The only downfall of the scheme was the rating agencies' overreliance on the government subsidy, which ultimately led to the closure of many SME credit rating units once the subsidy was retracted.

It should be noted that even though the scheme was a success in terms of its effectiveness to SMEs, there were still limited levels of coverage relative to the number of SMEs within the country. The scheme rated around 280,000 SMEs when fully operational, which is relatively large in traditional credit rating terms but is still quite low when we consider the total number of SMEs in India.[20] On a relative basis, the public sector rating unit at Banque de France has managed to rate around 3,00,000 SMEs out of a total of roughly 4,000,000 SMEs in the country, which is significantly larger on a per capita basis.

[20] India has one of the largest number of MSMEs in the world, which is roughly 63,380,000 with 99% of them being micro-enterprises; more here: Ministry of Micro, Small, and Medium Enterprises. (2022). Ministry of Micro, Small, And Medium Enterprises- Annual Report 2021–2022. [Online]. Ministry of Micro, Small, and Medium Enterprises. https://msme.gov.in/sites/default/files/MSMEENGLISHANNUALREPORT2021-22.pdf (Accessed 12 October 2023).

Of the 63,380,000 MSMEs, roughly, 13,800,000 are registered entities, more here: Statista. (2023). Number of registered MSMEs in India as of February 2023, by type. [Online]. Statista. https://www.statista.com/statistics/1384894/india-number-of-registered-msmes-by-type/#:~:text=As%20of%20February%202023% (Accessed 12 October 2023).

One of the issues with the ecosystem/subsidised model is that it is problematic from a political standpoint to have the government grant provided indefinitely.[21] This implies that the private sector ecosystem might need to be structured differently to ensure its long-term viability, which is discussed in detail in chapter nine. For countries wanting widespread credit rating coverage, the public sector model might be a viable alternative, providing much more scale and a sustainable long-term solution that the private sector could still complement. The rest of this section then unpacks the public sector model in greater detail and showcases why this might actually be a viable value proposition.

5.3 The Benefits of a Public Sector SME Credit Rating Agency

Whilst the author is generally a proponent of the private sector and its ability to service most sectors of the economy efficiently, he believes that, in certain circumstances, there is a requirement for government intervention. This is particularly true in the SME credit rating industry due to the significant benefits these ratings can provide and the reluctance of the private sector to provide these services due to profitability concerns. A public sector entity would look out for the best interests of SMEs, and due to their post-COVID-19 focus on this sector, it would ensure that the needs of these entities are adequately taken care of. Furthermore, and importantly, the public sector will not be entirely profit-driven, which would be advantageous due to the low levels of profitability associated with these ratings. Other broader benefits could be considered, such as the economic contributions of these ratings to GDP over the medium-long run. Within the project that Credit Rating Analytics is involved in with an emerging market country, we have projected that the contribution to GDP over the first five years would be in the region of $30 billion. When looked at from this perspective, this contribution dwarfs the outlay costs to establish the organisation, its operational costs, and the low-profit nature of the operation. The private sector might not look at it from this perspective, which is an important consideration and a motivating factor as to why the public sector could be ideally suited.

Furthermore, other unprofitable SME rating segments such as SME gradings, SME due diligence ratings, and ESG ratings have a higher propensity to

[21] The credit rating industry is at times cast in a negative light and it can become difficult from a political perspective to provide a grant which increases this sector's profitability, it is more palatable for the grant to be issued for a specific period.

be rolled out by a state entity on a country-wide basis. Similar to SME credit ratings, these ancillary ratings operate on low or lower profit margins, which creates a reluctance by the private sector to provide these services. These ratings can greatly benefit SMEs; however, it is unfortunate that they are not available in most countries. If we take Africa as an example, the due diligence rating function can be a game changer within the African Continental Free Trade Area. This is because cross-border business is sometimes inhibited by a lack of information on counterparty companies, thereby creating doubt about the legitimacy of doing business with these entities. A public sector SME due diligence offering could thus solve this by providing these ratings on the basis of how beneficial it would be from an economic perspective and its ability to boost exports from the SME space. There are also working examples of the European public sector model and its effectiveness. These examples are then first-hand evidence of why the public sector model is a viable solution.

Lastly, the public sector rating agency would be interested in the socioeconomic benefits that growth in the SME sector would bring about. This is important as many of these socioeconomic benefits are currently major areas of focus for governments, and the public sector rating agency could be the ideal platform to address some of these issues. The public sector would be willing to absorb some of the costs of doing this, which might not be the case within the private sector model. Within the project that Credit Rating Analytics is busy with, the government is creating a value proposition which is specifically aligned with the needs of female-owned SMEs. This would significantly benefit female-owned SMEs, which are more disadvantaged when accessing credit. However, it can be argued that if the public sector were not involved, there would be no incentive for the private sector to take the lead on this. The profit-driven nature of the private sector can sometimes increase the disparities these underrepresented groups face. This is one of the reasons the project that Credit Rating Analytics is busy with was created, as there needed to be a direct government intervention that could directly benefit female-owned businesses within that country.

References

Bartels, J. (2012). Bertelsmann Foundation Releases Blueprint for INCRA – An International Non-Profi. [Online]. BIAA. https://www.biia.com/bertelsmann-foundation-releases-blueprint-for-incra-an-international-non-profit-credit-rating-agenc (Accessed 6 September 2023).

Luitel, P, & Vanpee, R. (2018). How Do Sovereign Credit Ratings Help to Financially Develop Low-Developed Countries? https://papers.ssrn.com/sol3/papers.cfm?abstract_id=3287881 (Last accessed 2 September 2023).

Ministry of Micro, Small and Medium Enterprises. (2015). Performance and Credit Rating Scheme for Micro & Small Enterprises. [Online]. Ministry of Micro, Small and Medium Enterprises. https://msme.gov.in/sites/default/files/PCR_EN.pdf (Accessed 1 June 2023).

6

Practical Applications of the Public Sector SME Credit Rating Model and its Associated Benefits

6.1 The Public Sector Model in Use: The European Experience

As discussed in the section above, the European example remains the most successful attempt at creating a public sector credit rating agency. The central banks in Europe that have adopted the model have done so to create In-house Credit Assessment Systems (ICASs). These ICASs play a significant role within the Eurosystem collateral framework and have served as an effective tool to proliferate funding opportunities for SMEs. The value proposition of these SME credit rating units is in line with fully-fledged private sector SME credit rating agencies, and they have expanded their credit assessment capabilities by incorporating robust ESG rating methodologies.[1] The SME credit rating units utilize the subscription-based investor pays model, which does not permit direct credit rating requests from SMEs. Access to data on rated entities is available via a subscription service which is generally taken up by financial institutions, alternative lenders and related stakeholders who might be interested in this content. This operating model, coupled with the non-profit nature of these organisations, has resulted in these credit rating units being exempted from regulatory oversight by the European Securities

[1] The only difference with private sector SME credit rating agencies in Europe is the financial and operating model that is used, whereby the private sector rating agencies utilise an issuer pays model and accept direct rating requests from SMEs in contrast to the public sector who utilize the investor pays model.

S. Pillay, *The Next Frontier in SME Ratings*,
https://doi.org/10.1007/978-3-031-54015-8_6

and Market Authority (ESMA).[2] The SME credit rating unit at Banque de France formally requested an exemption from ESMA which was published in the Official Journal of the European Union on June 19th, 2010.[3] Although unregulated by ESMA, these SME credit rating units have robust compliance procedures and policies that, combined with the operating model, result in limited conflicts of interest or run-ins with the law. These entities were created to fulfil a regulatory function; however, they have evolved into fully-fledged SME credit rating agencies that provide a vital service to SMEs within the region.

6.2 A Case Study on Banque de France's Credit Rating Unit (The Largest SME Credit Rating Operation in the World)

The credit rating unit at Banque de France is an exemplary example of the ability of the public sector to create a viable credit rating agency that is widely accessible and highly regarded by end users. Banque de France houses the largest SME credit rating agency in the world (public or private), which has positively impacted French SMEs' ability to tap into traditional and non-traditional funding pools. The rating unit focuses exclusively on non-financial companies and utilizes a decentralized analyst team due to the sheer size of the organization and the different regions that require coverage. The ratings reflect BdF's assessment of an entity's ability to meet its financial commitments over the short to medium term (1–3 years), and these ratings are available on their exclusive FINBEN platform.[4] SME ratings are conducted on SMEs which have a turnover equal to or greater than EUR 750,000 with coverage on roughly 300,000 companies, 90% of which are SMEs. BdF adopts the investor pays model whereby investors pay an annual subscription to access their credit rating coverage.

---

[2] The credit rating regulations put forward by ESMA are viewed as the global gold standard as most countries throughout the world model their regulatory frameworks on those put forward by ESMA. Obtaining a regulatory waiver is then a testament to the faith placed by ESMA in the viability of this credit rating model and its ability to provide credit ratings in a just, viable and sustainable manner.

[3] Rating platform. (2022). Banque de France FIBEN. [Online]. Ratingplatform. https://www.ratingplatform.com/agency_view.php?id=45 (Accessed 5 March 2022).

[4] Banque de France. (2020). The Informational Value of Credit Ratings in the Bank/firm Relationship. [Online]. Banque de France. https://publications.banque-france.fr/sites/default/files/medias/documents/bdf227-3_credit_ratings_vf.pdf (Accessed 10 September 2023).

The methodology used to rate SMEs is quite sophisticated in nature and incorporates a "theme-based catch-up mechanism".[5] This approach utilises both a statistical and qualitative assessment. The credit rating system is segregated into three sub-models catering to small, larger, and consolidated groups. It is important to note that BdF utilizes sector-specific methodologies, which are the cornerstone of the SME rating concept. They identify seven economic sectors for the first two sub-groups, while an additional five sectors are utilized for the consolidated group sub-model. This is a significant value-add relative to the approach taken by commercial lenders, which, in most instances, do not incorporate a large number of industry-specific credit rating models.[6] The rating procedure is broken up into three stages, which are as follows (Table 6.1).

Table 6.1 The rating process at Banque de France

Stage	Further elaboration
The first stage involves a quantitative analysis based on a statistical rating model that uses balance sheet data, which involves the following four steps:	• A variable selection process • An optimisation algorithm that clusters the selected financial ratios into four themes and splits each ratio into multiple risk classes • A penalised logistic regression with coefficient adjustments that estimate an unbiased probability of default (PD) of non-financial companies (NFC) • The final step relates the underlying PD with a rating class (i.e., statistical rating) by defining a master scale based on the inverse function of a smoothing cubic spline and an optimisation algorithm
The second stage involves a qualitative analysis:	• BDF creates qualitative profiles for each company by conducting an expert assessment that complements the financial statistical ratings, allowing the rating to either be confirmed, upgraded, or downgraded
The final stage involves an additional qualitative analysis (based on specific events or the automatically collected characteristics of the company)	• Each company's extra-financial contributions are compiled, and their impact is statistically predetermined. A degree of flexibility is granted to the expert, who may sometimes modify the rating assigned in the previous steps to produce the global rating

Source Banco de España Eurosistema (2021)

[5] European Central Bank. (2021). Overview of Central Banks' In-house Credit Assessment Systems in the Euro Area. [Online]. European Central Bank. https://www.ecb.europa.eu/pub/pdf/scpops/ecb.op284~bbce5257bf.en.pdf (Accessed 5 December 2023).

[6] Although many banks have made a concerted effort to improve their credit scoring capabilities, a large number still use uniform credit assessment tools which cover multiple industries. This simplifies the credit rating process and reduces costs but decreases the inherent accuracy of these credit assessments.

The underlying models are calibrated using a five-year rolling window of financial statements and historical default data. The ratings handed out within the SME segment have been utilized for both direct lending and alternative lending activities, such as in the SME minibond market and within structured note issuances. The use of these ratings within the alternative funding channels showcases the underlying level of sophistication with these ratings and the associated trust that market participants have in the value proposition. The SME credit rating unit at Banque de France is, however, complemented by other government-backed initiatives which boost SME lending; some of the other notable initiatives are as follows (Table 6.2).

6.3 The Impact and Empirical Success of the Public Sector SME Credit Rating Model (We Showcase How SME Borrowing Activity Differs in Countries With and Without a Public Sector SME Credit Rating Industry)

The public sector SME credit rating model in France is not just successful in terms of its effective coverage of a large portion of the SME sector in France; it has also been successful in terms of its ability to assist the country to rank as one of the best performers in terms of access to credit to the. As evident from some of the graphs below, France ranks at either number one or in the top percentile for most lending metrics linked to the SME sector. The SME credit rating unit and other interventions within the SME space play a major role in these impressive lending statistics. It is also not an anomaly that the country with the largest SME credit rating agency simultaneously has some of the best SME lending statistics in the world.[7] Some of the lending statistics that stand out and commentary around how this SME credit rating unit plays an important role in this process can be found in the infographics below (Figs. 6.1 and 6.2).

As per the two graphs above, France has an extremely low SME loan rejection rate of just over 2% and is the lowest amongst OECD countries in the given sample population. While other government interventions have improved the lending statistics, the SME credit rating unit has played a major role. France's SME loan rejection rates are also significantly lower than those

[7] France has had many policy interventions within the SME space, however, the SME credit rating unit at Banque de France is one of the largest.

Table 6.2 Some of the notable initiatives which complement the SME credit rating unit

Initiative	Further elaboration
1. A vast database of the financial statements of SMEs	• It is mandatory for SMEs in France to publish their financial statements or face the repercussions of paying a penalty.[8] Access to quality financial inputs is a major requirement within the credit rating industry, and access to such data by the central bank makes the rating process much easier. Based on previous work that the author has completed within this space, private sector SME credit rating agencies often bemoan the lack of quality data inputs, especially with smaller firms within the SME space
2. The Central *Credit Register*	• Having a well-functioning national credit registry is a major benefit to France's public sector rating agency. The credit records of rated entities make up a small portion of their overall credit rating; however, this is an important component that adds to the accuracy of the SME ratings they provide
3. The national collateral registry	• The information asymmetry related to both fixed and movable collateral has been singled out as a major impediment to SME lending. The sophisticated collateral registry in France is a major benefit to the SME credit rating process as it allows the credit rating unit to have a 360^0 view of both movable and immovable collateral of rated entities

(continued)

[8] PWC. (2012). Doing Business in France. [Online]. PWC. https://www.pwc.de/de/internationale-maerkte/assets/doing-business-in-france.pdf (Accessed 1 September 2023).

Table 6.2 (continued)

Initiative	Further elaboration
4. The SME loan mediation service	• The loan mediation service indirectly assists the SME credit rating function as it increases the borrowing outcomes of rated entities and thus increases the effectiveness of these ratings. Mediating for rated entities becomes much easier as the central bank is in a position to leverage the in-depth understanding of rated SMEs. This service then accentuates the borrowing outcomes of rated entities and contributes to the success of the SME credit rating industry

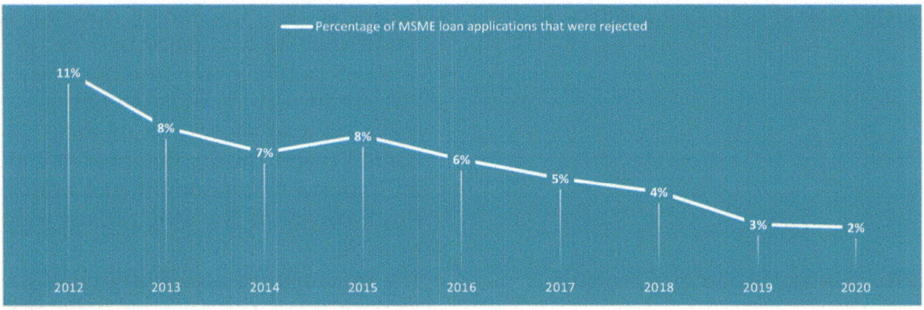

Fig. 6.1 The SME loan rejection rate in France (*Source* OECD [2022])

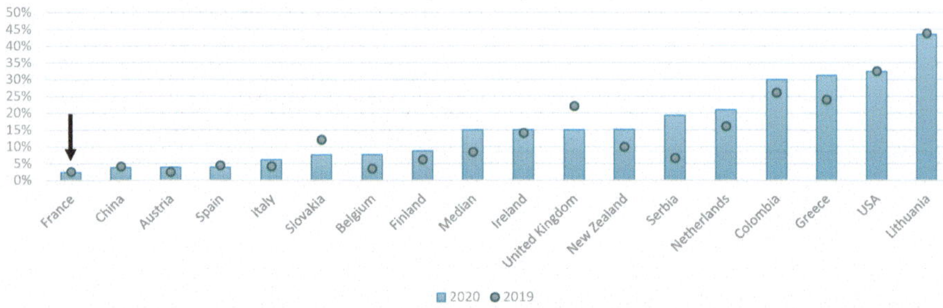

Fig. 6.2 SME loan rejection rates relative to other countries (*Source* OECD [2022])

of other OECD countries that do not have an SME credit rating industry (public or private). For example, the USA, which does not have a public or private sector SME credit rating industry, has an SME loan rejection rate of over 30%.[9] What is important to note is that the other government interventions have complemented the SME credit rating unit in bringing down the SME loan rejection rate. The SME loan mediation service, in particular, has played a significant role on this front and, together with the rating agency, has helped the rejection rate to decrease from roughly 11% in 2012 to 2% in 2020. Apart from the impressive SME loan rejection rate, the country has greatly compressed the interest charged to large companies versus SMEs/VSMEs. This is evident from the graph below (Fig. 6.3).

The interest rate differential between large and small enterprises is significant within emerging markets and is often a common grievance amongst SMEs. SMEs would naturally be charged a higher interest rate as their operating and financial profile would differ from larger firms; the problem arises when there is an unjustified divergence in the interest rate spread between these organisations. In the aftermath of the global financial crisis, France has managed to make significant strides in reducing the interest rate differential and, thus, reducing the borrowing rates of SMEs/VSMEs. Evidently, in the graph above, the interest rate difference between large, small, and very small businesses was in the region of 15% in 2008; fast forward to 2021, and that difference is under 5%. Favourable monetary policy and excess liquidity were also contributing factors to the compression of interest rates amongst segments; however, the decreased information asymmetry as a result of SME credit ratings cannot be ignored. It should be noted that on a relative basis,

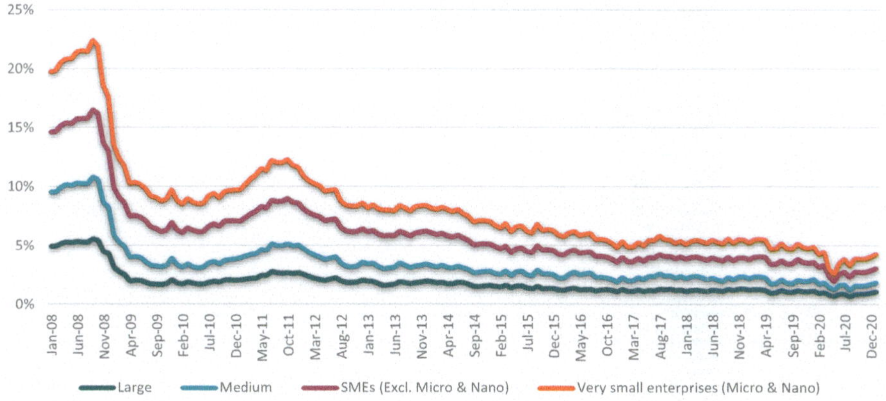

Fig. 6.3 The interest rate differential between smaller and larger firms (*Source* OECD [2022])

[9] The United States does have an SME credit scoring industry provided by the likes of Dun & Bradstreet. However, credit scoring, together with credit bureau reports, should not be confused with the SME credit rating concept.

SMEs in France are, on average, charged one of the lowest interest rates, according to Fig. 6.4.

Evidently, France comes in at number one across all countries within the graph in terms of the average interest charged to SMEs. However, caution will be given to the fact that interest rates within the Eurozone were at record lows over the observed period. Nevertheless, SMEs in France still fared far better than SMEs in other European countries, which faced similar macroeconomic conditions. This should be viewed as a huge success story in terms of France's overall approach to alleviating funding issues within the SME sector. The country's policies, as a collective, have been dynamic and effective at achieving its intended mandate. The strategy can be viewed as an access-to-finance ecosystem approach as other services, such as the SME loan mediation service, have worked concurrently to produce these exemplary lending statistics. The SME loan mediation service would likely have contributed to the low interest rates charged to SMEs, as one of its mandates is to ensure that SMEs are not charged exorbitant interest rates. However, the SME credit rating function has played an enabling role in these mediation activities due to its ability to supply the mediation service with in-depth information on rated entities. Furthermore, one should be aware that the development and

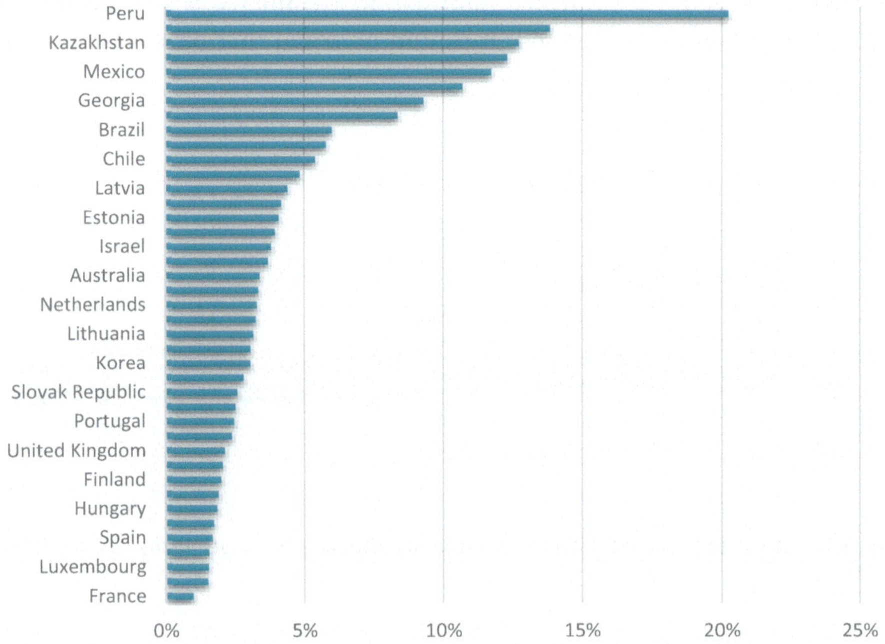

Fig. 6.4 Interest rates charged to MSMEs across the globe (2020) (*Source* OECD [2022])

growth of the SME credit rating unit at Banque de France has also coincided with the country boasting one of the lowest SME collateral requirements for borrowing purposes, coming in significantly lower than other countries within the graph below (Fig. 6.5).

SME collateral requirements are one of the significant impediments to access to finance and are typically caused by the information asymmetry between borrowers and lenders.[10] This results in lenders not having a concise understanding of the business in question and, therefore, requiring collateral for borrowing purposes. Thus, the low collateral requirements in France significantly benefit SMEs and add to the overall low levels of SME loan rejections (Fig. 6.6).

Lastly, a major issue regarding SMEs in most countries is the level of SME bankruptcies that occur within the initial operating years and when there are exogenous shocks to the economic system.[11] Whilst SME bankruptcies are common in all countries, the growth rate of these figures in France amid the COVID-19 pandemic was impressive relative to other countries. Access to finance directly linked to liquidity and solvency issues is one of the primary drivers behind SME bankruptcy rates, and the SME credit rating unit has

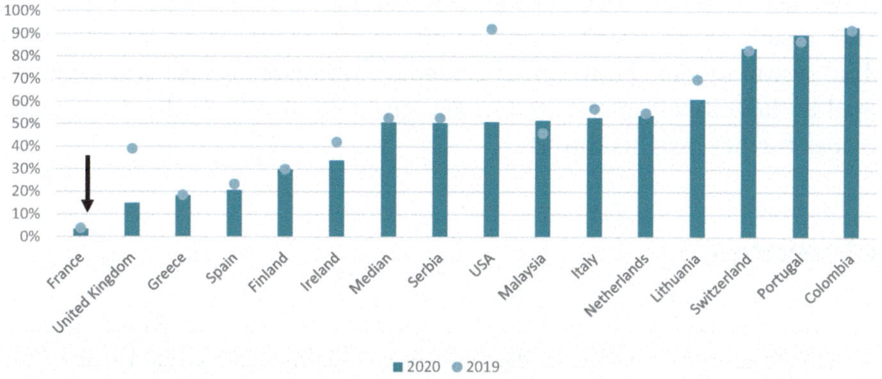

Fig. 6.5 Percentage of SMEs needing collateral to obtain finance (*Source* OECD [2022])

[10] SME owners utilise existing savings when establishing their businesses and, even once established, might not have the requisite amount of collateral that is required when raising capital.

[11] In the US, for example, it is estimated that 21.7% of businesses fail in the first year, less than 50% survive past year 5, and 33,3% of businesses survive past the ten-year mark. As indicated in Chapter Two, the figures are much worse for developing countries. More insights can be found here: SBF. (2020). Top Reasons for Small Business Success and Failure Rates. [Online]. Small Business Funding. https://www.smallbusinessfunding.com/small-business-success-and-failure-rates/ (Accessed 1 June 2023).

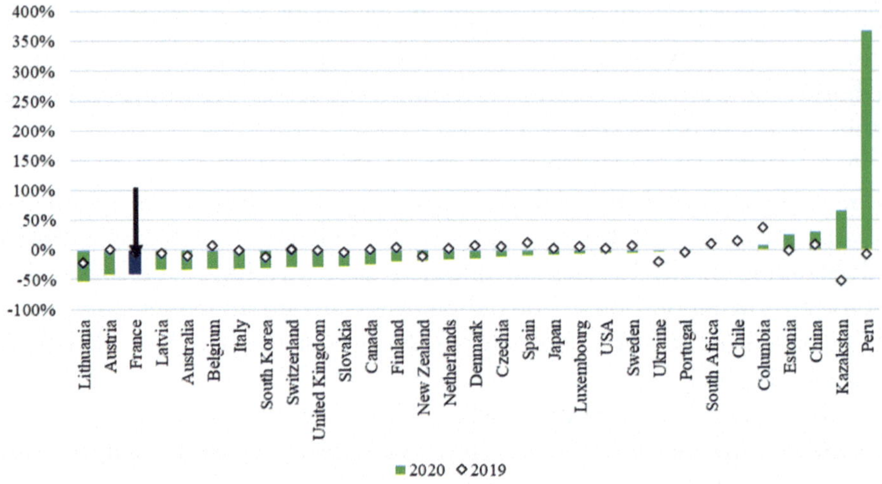

Fig. 6.6 The growth in the level of SME bankruptcy rates in France (*Source* OECD [2022])

contributed to improving access to finance and thus inhibiting the growth rate in SME bankruptcies.

The benefits showcased within this chapter and the empirical studies within chapter four provide a compelling argument for the adoption of the public sector model. However, the model's ultimate success will be determined by how it is implemented in any given country, and the next chapter provides further insights into this.

References

Banco de España Eurosistema. (2021). Overview of Central Banks' In-house Credit Assessment Systems in the Euro Area. [Online]. Banco de España Eurosistema. https://www.bde.es/f/webbde/SES/Secciones/Publicaciones/PublicacionesSeriadas/DocumentosOcasionales/21/Files/do2131e.pdf (Accessed 21 March 2022).

OECD. (2022). Financing SMEs and Entrepreneurs 2022: An OECD Scoreboard. *OECD Publishing*. https://doi.org/10.1787/e9073a0f-en

7

Bringing the Public Sector SME Credit Rating Concept into Fruition

7.1 Recommendations on How to Initiate the Development of a Public Sector SME Credit Rating Agency

The creation of any new public sector entity is an arduous task in itself, and given the legal implications of a credit rating agency, the notion of creating a public sector credit rating agency becomes a complex process.[1] As indicated in the previous chapters, there have been multiple attempts at creating a public sector credit rating agency that focuses on traditional rating concepts; however, all of these attempts have failed due to the legal, financial, and operational feasibility of establishing these organisations.[2] The author's firm has a consulting solution geared towards creating these public sector entities, and details of this solution are presented in this section. A broad overview of the different steps that are practically applied when attempting to create these organisations can be found below:

- Step 1: Capacity building with governments in different regions.

[1] Many failed attempts at creating these organisations have stemmed from the legal implications that could arise and the reluctance of the public sector to take on these potential risks.

[2] Some of these projects are ongoing, so there is still a possibility that a public sector rating agency focusing on the traditional credit rating industry can be established.

S. Pillay, *The Next Frontier in SME Ratings*,
https://doi.org/10.1007/978-3-031-54015-8_7

- Step 2: Internal engagements on the concept's viability and the creation of working committees dedicated to exploring the concept's merits; this would be done by the ministry linked to the SME sector.
- Step 3: Engaging with service providers who are skilled in the subject area and can assist with the different phases of the project.
- Step 4: Compiling a research report on the country aligned with the SME rating concept.
- Step 5: Conducting a pre-feasibility study.
- Step 6: Conducting a comprehensive feasibility study.
- Step 7: Designing working prototypes of the proposed entity's financial, operational, legal, and strategic models.
- Step 8: The pilot phase of the project.
- Step 9: The research and feedback phase, which measures the effectiveness of the project's pilot phase.
- Step 10: The implementation phase of the project.

Step 1: Capacity building with governments in different regions

As per the infographic above, the first step in this process should involve efforts by multilateral organisations or experts to upskill governments on the concept of SME credit ratings and how it can be implemented via a public sector model. Although very effective, one of the major shortfalls related to the SME credit rating concept is the lack of awareness around these ratings, as evidenced by many first-hand interactions that the author has had with public sector bodies. Increased awareness should naturally lead to elevated levels of interest, which could then lead to projects being initiated. Multilaterals such as the World Bank Group have initiated projects that are designed to increase awareness of the concept and ultimately increase the availability of these ratings. Credit Rating Analytics were assigned as advisors to the World Bank Group on this concept, and the public sector model was one of the options that we identified as a viable solution to provide these ratings on a wide-scale basis. Reference should also be made to the report completed within the World Bank project as it can be used as an excellent starting point to get upskilled on the concept and the public sector model.[3] Regional or continental-wide events would be effective at showcasing the concept as well as success stories in other regions. Furthermore, discussing success stories can be an optimal way of getting a buy-in from potential adopters of the model,

[3] The report that Credit Rating Analytics completed for the World Bank Group: IFC. (2024). The Global Survey Of SME Credit Rating Agencies. IFC.

as it will provide a first-hand account of the concept and what has and has not worked when attempting to bring it to fruition.

Step 2: Internal engagements on the concept's viability and the creation of working committees dedicated to exploring the concept's merits; this would be done by the ministry linked to the SME sector.

Once a country shows interest in the concept, there should be internal discussions on the merits of introducing the SME rating concept coupled with the public sector model. These discussions will involve ministries linked to the SME sector, the country's central bank, and the ministry tasked with trade and economic development. These key stakeholders can share their views on the concept and their initial thoughts on the prospects of introducing it into the country. Themes such as access to finance, access to market, and the global competitiveness of SMEs should form the basis of these discussions. The ministry linked to the SME sector should initially champion this initiative and take the lead on the future development of the concept. Multilateral organisations skilled in the subject matter could participate in these initial discussions as they can assess how effective the concept might be. A working committee should be formed to oversee the concept's initial development. This working committee can then lead the initiative and seek out additional stakeholders that could add value to the initial stages of the project.

Step 3: Engaging with service providers who are skilled in the subject area and can assist with the different phases of the project.

Step three would involve engaging with both private and public sector entities that are knowledgeable about the subject matter. The ministry linked to the SME sector, which champions the concept, can unpack its understanding of the concept and obtain expert advice from both the private and public sectors. Public sector entities currently providing these services or who have already started developing a public sector rating agency can then share their expert insights.[4] These insights would clarify how to get the concept off the ground, which stakeholders to engage with, and a run-down of some of the challenges that could be experienced.

[4] The public sector entities in Europe that currently provide these services should be the first port of call as they might be willing to provide guidance and have the requisite experience in this subject area.

Step 4: Compiling a research report on the country aligned with the SME rating concept.

The next step is important and involves conducting thorough research on the SME sector with a particular focus on concepts and themes which are linked to the SME rating sector. The four major themes linked to the SME rating concept are access to finance, access to market, the ability of SMEs to export goods and services, and the global competitiveness of these entities. This research report would then contextualise how the country is currently performing with regard to these themes and provide more clarity on the need or urgency to establish a public sector rating agency. This research report would also be key to the later stages of the project as it will provide a worthwhile economic assessment of the country.

Step 5: Conducting a pre-feasibility study on whether to introduce the concept into the country.

If there is firm interest after thoroughly researching and understanding the concept, the next step would be to map out a strategic plan on how to research the concept further. The first step within this strategic plan would be to conduct a pre-feasibility study on the concept, which could be done internally or outsourced to an expert with specialist knowledge.[5] The pre-feasibility study would examine whether the concept should be introduced into the country and whether the public sector model would be a viable solution. The important things to consider within the pre-feasibility study are:

- The market consensus as to whether the SME rating concept should be introduced and if key market participants would support the public or private sector model.
- A comparison between the pros and cons of introducing the public sector model versus creating a private sector industry. An analysis should also be made on the prospects of introducing both models (public and private).
- The legal implications of the public sector model on a relative basis to creating a private sector industry.

[5] Engaging with a third party might be beneficial in that the feasibility study would be free from bias and provide an independent opinion on if, when, and how a potential public sector rating agency should be established. The independent third party would look at things from a different perspective, and the recommendations put forward would come across as being more credible. This should be important when trying to get a buy-in from other related stakeholders.

- The operational implications.
- The financial implications.
- The economic and socioeconomic benefits of the proposed rating agency.
- The strategic implications.
- Decisioning on whether to introduce the public, private, or both models into the country.
- A concise strategic overview of how to go about completing the rest of the project.

This is a vital exercise as it demonstrates to stakeholders that the government has not jumped into the concept but has assiduously explored the viability of these ratings and the operating model that should be introduced.[6] With the emerging market country that Credit Rating Analytics is working with, the pre-feasibility study has proven to be a valuable exercise as it has showcased the potential economic and socioeconomic benefits of the concept as well as the potential demand for these ratings. Many countries often jump into projects that seem promising but subsequently face roadblocks from various stakeholders when they realise that there weren't any comprehensive landscape studies done to warrant the development of the concept in question. Allowing a third party to conduct the feasibility study is also advantageous as it eliminates any existing biases and allows for an independent assessment of whether or not the concept should be introduced. Once the pre-feasibility study is completed, it is then advisable to have a stakeholder engagement session in which the findings from the pre-feasibility study are presented. The stakeholder session will be a great opportunity to engage in an open discussion on the merits of the concept and concerns of various stakeholders. Feedback from the session can be incorporated into the comprehensive feasibility study, which is the next step in this process.

Step 6: Completing a comprehensive feasibility study.

A comprehensive feasibility study would be the next step should the pre-feasibility study's findings be affirmative. This comprehensive feasibility study would build on the findings from the pre-feasibility study and unpack these concepts in greater detail. It would follow a similar format but would differ in the following way:

[6] Countries often jump into concepts which seem great on paper and sometimes are; however, problems arise at later points, and these projects stall if it is brought up that the proper feasibility studies were not completed. This could be in the form of political pushback or opponents to the idea; it is then best to conduct comprehensive feasibility studies at the onset.

- The primary research collection would be much more comprehensive and involve engagements with a larger number of stakeholders. This would include (not limited to) banks, microfinance institutions, private equity firms, venture capital, angel investors, SME debt and equity exchanges, large non-financial firms that can procure from SMEs, individual SMEs, key departments within other ministries and agencies, key departments within the central bank, development banks, multilateral organisations, and civil society.[7] These engagements would seek to determine the demand for the services of the potential rating agency, how it should be set up and any additional recommendations.
- In-depth financial modelling on the costs to establish the public sector rating agency. This will entail forecasting the financial performance over the initial operational years to determine the initial outlay costs to establish the organisation. Additional economic modelling can be conducted as it is important to showcase how the potential economic benefits measure up to the initial financial costs.
- An in-depth operational feasibility study.
- A comprehensive analysis of all of the legal implications involved in getting the proposed rating agency fully operational. This is important as the legal implications of a public sector model have been one of the major impediments to establishing a public sector rating agency.
- Decisioning on whether to introduce the public sector rating agency into the country and the urgency of doing so. Suggestions should also be provided on the project's next steps and a roadmap to how the organisation could be created if the feasibility study is affirmative.
- The feasibility of introducing ancillary services such as the SME loan mediation and the grading preparation program.

The findings from the feasibility study will then be utilised in all of the subsequent phases of the project and will form the basis of the project's design phase.

Step 7: The design phase of the organisation.

If the comprehensive feasibility study indicates that the rating agency should be established, the next step will involve designing the proposed entity. The stakeholder feedback received within the comprehensive feasibility study will

[7] It is important to engage with a large audience as they would provide contrasting views, which would assist when determining if and how the public sector rating agency should be set up.

be used, and additional engagements with other key stakeholders can complement this. The takeaway from this phase of the project is to create working prototypes that can then be seamlessly implemented. It is also important to pilot these concepts within the design phase and subsequently re-design these prototypes based on the feedback provided. The prototypes could be segregated as follows:

1. A prototype for the operational model that the proposed organisation will utilise.
2. A prototype for the financial model.
3. A prototype for the legal and compliance configuration of the proposed organisation.

The design phase is really important as it creates a blueprint of how the organisation will be structured once it is operationalized.

Step 8: The pilot phase of the project

The next phase would entail piloting these ratings prior to the final prototype and implementation phase. A theoretical design would be great; however, practically testing this theoretical concept would be a pragmatic approach to determine what works and does not work. Within the pilot phase, sample pilot sites would be strategically selected, and SMEs would be rated within these regions.[8] The public sector rating agency would need to pay a private sector firm to convert these prototypes into temporary workable solutions which would be capable of handing out these ratings. This would be in particular reference to the rating methodology, the rating tool that will be used, and any other related IT tools that would be needed to roll out these ratings. The pilot phase will incorporate the rating process outlined within the design phase and will be a necessary test of how that process can be further streamlined.

Compliance would be essential in the project's pilot phase due to the potential legal liabilities arising from using these ratings. There would then need to be clearly defined legal liability clauses exempting these pilot ratings from any legal liabilities. It can be taken a step further by entering into service-level agreements with participating banks that might accept these

[8] The pilot sites should be done in areas which have a large concentration of diverse SMEs spread across various sectors. The pilot sites should also correlate with the sites that would be chosen for the initial rollout of the ratings, as it will provide important insights on what to expect, thereby facilitating a smoother rollout of these services.

ratings; these service-level agreements could mention the nature of the pilot phase and the discretion that would need to be applied by end users of these ratings. The SMEs within the pilot phase could be SMEs with a track record with the agency/entity tasked with managing the public sector rating agency. This would then increase the authenticity of the ratings and reduce the probability of engaging with SMEs, which might provide unreliable data inputs, resulting in inaccurate rating assessments and inefficient capital allocations. An important step in this process would be obtaining regulatory approval and receiving feedback on the best way to pilot these ratings.

Step 9: The research and feedback phase measures the effectiveness of the project's pilot phase.

The final phase prior to implementation would be conducting research to determine how effective these ratings have been within the pilot phase. The research will effectively investigate how these ratings have impacted SMEs' ability to access credit or secure new business opportunities. It will involve surveying rated entities and getting their direct feedback on this; the collected data will then be processed and reported on. These rated entities will also be probed on their experience with the rating process so that decisions can be made on how best to structure this process going forward. One of the key objectives will be to compare the research findings to the projections made during the feasibility studies to determine if the rating agency will have a similar economic and socioeconomic impact once it is established.

The insights gained from the research effort will serve as critical feedback, allowing the grading agency to re-design its operating and rating model to best serve the needs of related stakeholders.

Step 10: The implementation phase of the project.

The implementation phase will entail bringing the project to fruition and operationalizing the working prototypes to establish a fully-fledged public sector rating agency. This is the most important and difficult step of the process, and some of the key requirements to get the organisation operational are outlined below (Table 7.1).

Table 7.1 The key requirements to get the public sector SME credit rating agency off the ground

Key requirement	Further elaboration
Securing the requisite funding	Securing the requisite funding is one of the most important aspects of getting the rating agency off the ground. To effectively do this, the steps above must be carefully followed, as these steps will unlock the information and data required to bring funding partners on board. For example, the comprehensive feasibility study will provide important information related to the proposed entity's economic benefits, which would be important when getting a buy-in from potential investors and multilateral organisations. The same would be true about the financial feasibility study as it would provide an in-depth breakdown of how the funds will be utilised over the initial operating period and the organisation's earning potential. Getting the project up and running without any funding will not be possible, and the team behind the venture will need to have a clearly mapped out financing plan which defines the capital structure. Roadshow events will then need to be conducted to get the internal buy-in to secure funding from the country's Ministry of Finance/National Treasury. Similar roadshow events can be held with external shareholders, such as multilateral development banks, who could come on as strategic funders. The important approach with this would be to get potential funders on board during the initial phases of the project, as it will increase their awareness of the project and enhance the likelihood of getting a buy-in from them when approached for funding. The easiest way to do this would be to include these stakeholders as key participants within the data collection phases of the pre and comprehensive feasibility studies. The content from the design phase would also be key as it will include the prototypes of the final concept and results from the pilot phase.
Registering the proposed SME rating agency	Getting regulatory approval would be important and could be a complex process as the proposed entity would need to be registered with the regulator that oversees credit rating agencies within the country. We touch on this aspect in greater detail within the section below, which deals with the technical requirements to get the project functioning fully.

(continued)

Table 7.1 (continued)

Key requirement	Further elaboration
Getting the central bank's approval	The country's central bank would need to be brought in from the initial phases of the project as the activities of the proposed entity will directly affect macro-prudential risks. Getting the central bank's approval would then be important to bring the organisation to fruition. This task might be made easier if the credit rating agency is housed within the central bank, as is the case in Europe; however, the ownership structure will be determined within the feasibility and design phases of the project.
Assembling the board of directors	A capable and experienced board of directors might be a regulatory requirement and then done out of necessity, but it would nevertheless be essential to set up a board of directors to assist with oversight and the organisation's strategic direction. The board would need to be comprised of experienced directors who could provide strategic oversight to the organisation.
Service level agreements with private sector companies	These service-level agreements would be with private sector companies to which certain functions are outsourced. Moreover, these agreements would cover essential areas such as data protection and privacy as well as turnaround times for services provided. Some IT functions would need to be outsourced, and there would need to be comprehensive service-level agreements to ensure that services are carried out and in line with the strategic objectives of the public sector rating agency.

7.2 The Technical Requirements to Establish a Public Sector SME Credit Rating Agency

At first glance, and due to the limited availability of these ratings in the majority of countries, it is natural to believe that most countries would lack all of the in-house technical capabilities to create such an organisation. Whilst this might be true in many cases, it should be noted that this should not be an inhibiting factor as technical skills, which might be lacking, can be outsourced to the private sector.[9] One should be mindful that since there are no public sector SME rating agencies within emerging markets, the skill sets to create these organisations are limited. This is one of the reasons behind the decision to create the consulting solution at Credit Rating Analytics, which focuses on assisting countries with end-to-end support in establishing a public sector SME credit rating agency. The solution that we have created

[9] The public sector would naturally need to outsource some of the IT functions to third-party firms as they would not have many of the requisite systems.

allows countries to outsource the feasibility, design, pilot, and implementation phases of the project to an expert third-party firm. The government still works closely with Credit Rating Analytics during this period, and all of the work completed is per the government's and key stakeholders' specifications and needs. Credit Rating Analytics simply implements these specifications and adds our expert insights. The end objective of the consulting solution is to hand over a fully functional SME credit rating agency to the government.

The primary technical requirements are summarised in Table 7.2.

7.3 The Regulatory Considerations for a Public Sector SME Credit Rating Agency and What Needs to be Done for the Organisation to be Established

The regulatory considerations for a public sector credit rating agency are important as this has been a key impediment to establishing these entities in the past. Based on prior research by the author and his engagements with key stakeholders, the SME credit rating function is regulated using the same framework that governs traditional credit rating agencies.[10] These regulatory frameworks have become quite comprehensive in the aftermath of the global financial crisis. However, it can be argued that these updated or newly created regulations do not apply to the SME rating function and are not commensurate with the risks involved in rating these underlying securities. This can often be a problem for SME rating agencies due to the costs involved in abiding by these regulatory frameworks, which have contributed to the low levels of profitability within the industry. One of the recommendations that Credit Rating Analytics put forward in the World Bank Group project as well as other related projects, is for regulators to create bespoke regulatory frameworks for the SME rating function. These specific regulations would go a long way in reducing the overall regulatory costs and decreasing the probability of conflicts of interest, as the regulations would be better aligned with the underlying risks. The ministry linked to the SME sector that initiates the public sector SME rating project should proactively reach out to the regulators in the country to explore creating a specific regulatory framework. In most instances, no private sector SME credit rating industry will be in place,

[10] Credit Rating Analytics did provide some recommendations within the World Bank project on how bespoke regulatory frameworks can be created for the SME credit rating industry as there are currently none in place.

Table 7.2 Some of the technical requirements to establish and maintain a public sector credit rating agency

Requirement	Further elaboration
1. An understanding of the SME credit rating concept	This basic technical requirement can be obtained via capacity-building initiatives with experts on this subject area. If a public sector SME credit rating agency is established, the majority of staff members will be dealing with this concept for the first time. The capacity-building sessions might need to be structured to introduce the general credit rating concept first and thoroughly unpack the SME credit rating concept thereafter. This would be a strong approach as employees of the organisation might not be familiar with the credit rating concept in general. The subsequent upskilling and capacity-building can then focus on the public sector rating agency specifically and its business model, operating model, financial model, IT systems, and compliance-related matters.
2. A robust regulatory framework	A robust regulatory framework related to the SME rating concept will need to be implemented as this provides peace of mind to end users regarding the accuracy and authenticity of these ratings. A bespoke regulatory framework related to the SME credit rating concept would be ideal as it would deal specifically with the risks associated with this concept. Most countries with an underlying SME credit rating agency do not have a bespoke regulatory framework, as SME rating agencies have to adhere to the traditional credit rating framework. Within the project that Credit Rating Analytics completed for the World Bank Group, we provided recommendations on how such a framework could be structured and what variables need to be included. Incorporating such a framework could be highly advantageous to the success of the SME credit rating function and would then be an important underlying technical requirement. Due to the infancy stage of the concept, there is a high probability that the public sector rating agency will be the first to roll out these ratings within the country. Once there is clarity around the establishment of the organisation, the team setting up the public sector rating agency should proactively reach out to the regulators and work closely to design a framework to govern the concept in the country. This engagement should be done in a way that does not jeopardise the regulator's independence.

(continued)

Table 7.2 (continued)

Requirement	Further elaboration
3. A comprehensive SME credit rating methodology.	As indicated in the sections above, one of the primary advantages of the SME credit rating concept is its vast sets of industry and sub-industry-specific credit rating methodologies. These methodologies are viewed as the differentiating factor between the accuracy of these ratings relative to the credit-scoring models utilised by banks and other financial institutions. Having a robust set of properly back-tested and optimally weighted SME credit rating methodologies would then be imperative to the success of the proposed public sector rating agency. Developing these methodologies could be outsourced to a specialist private sector firm which focuses on SME methodology development and could be complemented by an in-house team to oversee the process. Historical default data is key to this process, so access to the relevant databases would be integral; these data sets could be obtained from financial institutions, risk consultancies, other credit rating agencies, or the central bank. The public sector rating agency would subsequently build up its repository of such datasets, which the internal risk department can manage and incorporate into the rating methodologies.
4. A robust credit rating platform.	The credit rating platform would form the core of the proposed public sector credit rating agency and will be utilised to conduct the rating process, access existing ratings, and maintain and update ratings. To ensure efficiencies, it would be ideal if the rating functionality is housed within a cloud-based tool. SME credit ratings across various jurisdictions have been compiled via Excel tools, which have worked; however, due to the scale of a public sector rating agency, this would need to be done via an online platform. The online platform should have the functionality to access, retrieve, and edit existing ratings quickly, securely, and efficiently. The platform should also have the functionality to allow third-party access, enabling them to log in and view existing ratings. The government in question can outsource the development of such a platform to a third party or create this internally.
5. An efficient CRM and ERP platform.	Due to the sheer quantum of ratings that will be handed out via the public sector model, the government must have a robust customer relations management (CRM) tool. The core function of the CRM tool is to manage the credit rating from initiation all the way through to completion and allow different stakeholders to work on the rating during this process. The tool will add significant efficiency to the overall credit rating process and form the backbone of the credit rating function. An Enterprise Resource Planning (ERP) tool will be required due to the sheer size of the organisation, its large staff complement, and its various departments.

(continued)

Table 7.2 (continued)

Requirement	Further elaboration
6. Efficient data storage and IT security.	As we continue transitioning into a digital environment, data privacy, and security are two of the core areas of focus which ensure that confidential client data is safe and used for its intended purpose. The public sector rating agency would then need to ensure that its data storage infrastructure is acceptable and that it abides by all data storage laws. Many countries have adopted policies around data storage, which specify the geographic locations where data centres should be located, and the proposed public sector rating agency would need to abide by that. The security around client data would also need to be of the highest standard, as the data would include confidential financial data of rated entities. Data breaches could have significant implications for the rating agency and jeopardise its viability if clients lose faith in its ability to store their data safely.
7. A well-structured internal compliance team.	Compliance within any credit rating agency is essential, and this is no different within an SME credit rating agency. The compliance function generally sits parallel to the rating agency and reports directly to the board of directors. The public sector rating agency would need to have a robust compliance division where the compliance function has been tailored to specifically prevent conflicts of interest that could arise. The compliance function should align with the organisation's code of conduct rules and international standards. Global bodies such as the International Organization of Securities Commissions (IOSCO) provide internationally accepted guidelines on best practices, which should be acknowledged and incorporated where applicable. The core focus should be on achieving globally accepted compliance standards, minimising and eliminating any conflicts of interest, and enhancing the underlying accuracy of credit ratings that are handed out. One of the major criticisms of the public sector credit rating model is the compliance issues and the propensity to hand out false credit ratings. It is then imperative that the compliance function is configured to reduce the probability of such practices from occurring. Due to the nature and importance of the compliance and regulatory function, we discuss this in greater detail in the section below.
8. An experienced and strategically assembled board of directors.	As previously discussed, the board of directors of the proposed public sector entity would be a core contributor to the sustainability and strategic growth of the organisation. Assembling a competent board with diverse backgrounds in the credit rating industry, financial markets, and the region would be imperative to its long-term success and viability. Due to the nature of the operation and the limited knowledge of this concept, it is important that the board of directors is set up at the onset of the organisation's development.

(continued)

Table 7.2 (continued)

Requirement	Further elaboration
9. A credit rating preparation unit	The previous section provided insights into what an SME credit rating preparation program is, and the author believes that it should be mandatory for most countries due to the informal nature of these entities.

so the government can take the lead on this initiative. This framework can be valuable should private sector SME credit rating agencies want to enter the market, as is the case in Europe, where there is a combination of private and public sector SME credit rating agencies. Having these bespoke regulatory frameworks provides additional peace of mind to the end users of these ratings that additional steps have been taken to ensure that these ratings are comprehensively regulated.

Moreover, the key considerations from a regulatory perspective are the in-house regulatory functions that will need to be created to ensure that the organisation abides by the required regulations and that there are limited conflicts of interest or run-ins with the law. It should be noted that a public sector initiative would result in a significant number of ratings being handed out, which would also increase the probability of run-ins with the law or conflicts of interest. Robust internal risk frameworks must be in place to prevent these occurrences and complement the organisation's code of conduct. Emphasis should be placed on the regulatory structure, which dictates the reporting structure of the regulatory function. The regulatory design will be done at inception and should be continuously updated to address additional risks. The regulatory function should be adequately staffed so that it can properly oversee the total number of ratings handed out. These services will then constitute a large amount of the organisation's overall costs, but this would be necessary to ensure that the ratings are free from conflicts of interest and accurately represent the intrinsic value of the underlying rated SMEs.

7.4 Key Considerations Related to the Operational Model of a Public Sector Credit Rating Agency

The operational model that will be deployed will form the organisation's core, and this section briefly covers some of the operational considerations. The author believes that whilst a large number of the operational considerations would be similar to that of any organisation, the prominent ones that are worth considering are as follows:

7.4.1 The Operational IT Requirements

One of the differences between the SME credit rating industry and the traditional credit rating industry comes down to different approaches related to the use of automation in the credit rating process. Within the SME credit rating industry, a concerted effort has been made to increase automation in order to reduce human capital requirements and costs. One of the failures we have witnessed is attempting to replicate the traditional credit rating model in the SME credit rating space. This has resulted in a labour-intensive operating model that does not align with the income generated from these SME ratings, which is significantly lower than the traditional credit rating industry. The rating agencies that have managed to become somewhat successful have integrated technology to a large extent and have reduced the number of analysts required to complete these ratings. Having a robust backend IT system is imperative to ensure that the rating agency operates efficiently and cost-effectively. As most countries will need to outsource this function, they must consider paying for this on a fixed-cost annual basis. This ensures that the IT costs remain affordable as variable IT costs could result in exorbitant IT spending as the number of ratings increases. Countries have attempted to enter into joint ventures with established private sector rating agencies, yet the approach has not translated into favourable outcomes. This is because the rating agencies are interested in profit maximisation, whereas governments are interested in providing the maximum amount of coverage at a fee that would be attractive to SMEs. The government would also consider pricing these ratings so that the overall organisation operates on a breakeven basis; however, this would only be possible if it does not enter into an equity-like joint agreement with a private sector credit rating agency. As IT requirements are the highest outsourced cost, careful consideration will need to be given as to how any arrangements will be structured. The author has encountered instances in which governments were keen on the public sector model, but the projects stalled when there was talk of a joint venture with the private sector firm, and the figures then seemed too exorbitant. The only IT cost with a level of variability would be the data storage costs, which increase as data storage increases. Utilising a fixed cost for the rating system with data storage variability would be the ideal approach to ensure the organisation's long-term viability and sustainability.

7.4.2 The Human Capital Constituency

Human capital is one of the most critical components of an SME credit rating agency (public or private), as they are involved in every step of the credit rating process. Human capital costs also make up the largest component of overall costs and are thus an important consideration when establishing a public sector rating agency. It is important to note that due to the infancy stage of the industry, the pool of highly skilled human capital staff in this subject area is scarce. The public sector rating agency would need to hire staff from related industries and engage in significant capacity-building to upskill them on the concept. These capacity-building initiatives could initially be outsourced to specialist third-party firms but could subsequently be done in-house once the organisation becomes experienced in this subject area. It should be noted that the human capital constituency will be quite large and based on the number of ratings handed out within a public sector model. Furthermore, regulatory considerations might determine the organisation's structure; for example, regulations could dictate the reporting structure of the regulatory unit as it is sometimes required to report directly to the board of directors. The organisation will then need to have a robust human capital structure that must be appropriately designed at inception.

7.4.3 Recommendations on an Optimal Financial Model

The financial model deployed by the rating agency is important as it will be directly linked to its long-term sustainability. There will need to be an income generation component within the value proposition, as it would be impractical to have the rating agency perpetually run off 100% government funding. As we have seen in most public sector initiatives, even if there is a significant public benefit, there is always a fee that is eventually charged to ensure the long-term viability of the public sector entity. This fee will, however, need to be structured so that it is affordable to SMEs, as these entities are often cost-conscious and find it difficult to part ways with their hard-earned money. When it comes to the credit rating industry, three primary financial models can be used: the investor pays model, the issuer-pays model, and a hybrid model. The investor pays model was the initial model used within the credit rating industry, which entailed investors paying a subscription fee to access credit rating data on a wide range of rated entities. The model is still used today but has lost its prevalence due to the more profitable issuer-pays model, which involves the rated entity paying to get rated. The issuer-pays model is the most widely used credit rating model and the dominant model within the SME credit rating industry. However, the model has received lots of negative criticism due to its propensity to attract conflicts of interest. Rating agencies view it as the most financially viable option within the SME space due to the industry's low-profit margins, and it can also be combined with the investor pays model to form a hybrid model. The hybrid model is quite popular and is adopted by a large number of SME credit rating agencies due to the demand from financial institutions to access quality data related to the credibility of SMEs. It provides a dual source of income, which is often welcomed and thus increases the long-term sustainability of these entities. The subscription-based income stream provides a bit more financial stability as it is less volatile and ensures somewhat of a guaranteed income stream. The author recommends that this financial model be deployed and that the public sector rating agency design a robust analytical platform to which end users can log in.[11]

The fee structure charged to SMEs requires significant attention, and the author recommends that the fee structure be on a sliding scale in which larger SMEs are charged a higher rating fee. Due to the cost sensitivity of SMEs, it is imperative to put in place an optimal and differentiated fee structure for each SME segment. The staggered fee structure worked well in India during the government-backed performance and credit rating scheme and is used by a large number of private sector SME credit rating agencies within different jurisdictions. Research into what fee structures could work can be done within the feasibility studies in which SMEs can be probed on their preferences. As previously mentioned, the organisation will, at a minimum, need to operate at a breakeven rate, and the fee structure will need to factor this in to ensure that it covers the operating costs. If the organisation goes ahead with the hybrid fee structure in which corporates pay to access the requisite rating data, these fees could be used to partially offset the low fees charged to rate individual SMEs. Large corporates are in a better position to absorb higher subscription fees, and this can be strategically set up to ensure that the fee charged to SMEs is affordable and results in sufficient demand for these ratings.

[11] This would, however, need to adhere to some regulatory frameworks as countries might stipulate how these financial models are structured and if there are any limitations considering that it is a public sector initiative.

7.4.4 The Strategic Considerations of Setting Up a Public Sector Rating Agency

Getting a buy-in to establish a public sector rating agency (traditional or SME) is no easy task due to the costs involved as well as the legal and operational implications. Identifying and highlighting the strategic benefits is paramount to ensure that relevant stakeholders see merit in establishing the organisation. Identifying these potential strategic benefits is also important to ensure that the organisation is designed to accentuate these strategic benefits. Some of the key strategic benefits to consider are as follows (Table 7.3).

Table 7.3 Aligning the strategic benefits of the proposed public sector rating agency with key stakeholders

Potential strategic alignment	Further elaboration
How does the proposed rating agency align with the government's primary strategic growth plans?	Most governments will have a long and medium-term strategic plan, which, in most instances, will include SME development. It is then essential to individually dissect all SME-related themes and identify how the proposed public sector rating agency can strategically align with these themes. Due to the adverse effects of the COVID-19 pandemic, a large number of governments have increased their focus on the SME space. Access to finance, access to market, and the ability of the SME sector to ease the unemployment burden are the major focus areas. A mapping should then be conducted around the individual actionable initiatives and how the SME rating concept can complement this. Apart from the direct linkages, focus should also be placed on the indirect socioeconomic strategic benefits. Government policy would naturally be aligned to alleviate some of these socioeconomic issues, and there should be an emphasis on how the SME rating concept can strategically complement these government policies.
How does the proposed rating agency align with the strategic objectives of a country's central bank as well as development banks (local and multilateral)?	The central banks of most countries have a mandate which covers economic growth. SME development is included in many of these growth initiatives, and central banks have specific programs linked to access to finance within the SME space. When attempting to establish an SME credit rating agency, it is essential to identify these programs and to highlight how a public sector SME credit rating agency can strategically benefit these programs. Development banks are also credited with having a mandate linked to SME development and related socioeconomic factors which are linked to the SME sector. These development banks include SME development within their long-term strategic plans and often have direct programs which target the SME sector. Identifying strategic synergies and then designing a value proposition aligning with this will be necessary.

(continued)

(continued)

Potential strategic alignment	Further elaboration
What are the strategic benefits of the proposed rating agency to individual SMEs?	When considering developing a public sector SME credit rating agency, the needs of individual SMEs would naturally rank the highest. Understanding these needs is critically important as it allows the public sector rating agency to be designed to align itself strategically to these needs. For example, business continuation and exit strategies are common issues for SMEs and are left largely unresolved, resulting in inefficient outcomes for individual SME owners and the economy at large. SME owners naturally value their businesses higher than their actual value and might become reluctant to sell or part ways with it when the business is in good standing. If that business owner gets ill with time, passes on, or wants to retire, the business's value or appeal might diminish, resulting in its eventual closure or sale at a much lower price. Understanding and acting on this need can result in a public sector rating agency including comprehensive business valuations in its rating reports. When included in a standard due diligence business report, these independent valuations can provide the business owner with an accurate, independent opinion on the business's fair value, which the business owner is more likely to accept. This can then facilitate the sale of the business and even assist the purchaser with securing funding to purchase the business. It is just one example of why it is important to understand the needs of SMEs within a country and then design the rating agency's value proposition to strategically align with these needs. A misalignment of these needs is one of the primary reasons SME rating agencies have proven unsuccessful, as it is assumed that these needs can be easily understood at face value. We discuss some of the other needs of individual SMEs within the section related to private sector SME credit rating agencies.
What are the key strategic benefits of the proposed rating agency to regional and continental-wide trade blocs?	Trade blocs and common trade areas are great initiatives that are typically underutilised due to factors the SME rating function can resolve. Independent, unbiased assessments of SMEs are not freely available in most of these trade blocs but can be a key strategic enabler if made readily available.[12] It is then important to understand these strategic linkages and outline them when trying to get the organisation off the ground. Within the project that Credit Rating Analytics is busy with, there are frequent references to how the proposed public sector grading agency will align with regional and continental-wide trade blocs. This is done to emphasise the untapped potential enhancements in trade which can be unleashed through the SME rating concept. Most governments' strategic planning focuses on how to increase the effectiveness of these trade blocs, so emphasising the benefits of the SME rating concept is pivotal when trying to get a buy-in for the concept.

[12] Many trade blocs are not operating optimally due to this deficiency, as businesses, individuals, or governments are reluctant to do business with smaller firms with which they are not familiar.

7.5 Insights Gained from Assisting an Emerging Market Country to Create the World's Largest Public Sector SME Grading Agency

As indicated in the sections above, Credit Rating Analytics has a bespoke consulting solution geared towards assisting sovereign states in creating public sector SME credit rating agencies. The consulting solution involves a step-by-step process in which we transition the public sector credit rating concept from the idea phase into a fully-fledged organisation. Some of the insights gained from the current project that we are working on are included in this section.[13] These insights might be helpful to countries that want to kick-start the development of a similar organization (Table 7.4).

Apart from the recommendations above, there also needs to be ancillary services which complement the overall value proposition. Having the SME credit rating concept in isolation might yield positive results, but this can be significantly enhanced if other ancillary services complement it.[14] Although we have introduced and discussed some of these ancillary services in the section above, Table 7.5 provides insights into how it was approached within the project that CRA is busy with:

[13] Credit Rating Analytics has been appointed as the lead advisor to an emerging market country wanting to create such an organisation. The project has a 2-year duration, after which we will hand over a fully functional public sector credit rating agency, more insights can be found here: Pillay, S., Ismail, Z., Sikochi, A., & Odii, C. (2023). Introduction to Business Government and International Economy (BGIE)—New Course Development. Harvard Business School. https://www.hbs.edu/faculty/Pages/item.aspx?num=65812 (Accessed 1 June 2024).

[14] One of the reasons that the private sector has not experienced significant demand is that SMEs might not see value in these ratings in their current form. Adding in these ancillary services increases the value that SMEs derive from these ratings which then boosts the long-term viability of the concept.

Table 7.4 Insights & recommendations gained from the existing project, which attempts to create a public sector credit rating agency

Insights & recommendations	Further elaboration
The public sector model can be used as an effective platform to address socioeconomic imbalances within a country.	Within the project that the author's firm is working on, the proposed public sector SME rating agency focuses explicitly on female-owned nMSMEs. The value proposition is designed to cater to the needs of female-owned nMSMEs and ensure that it is easily accessible to this demographic. Other countries wanting to create similar organisations can leverage the public sector's ability to do so and possibly follow a similar approach. This approach might be unique to the public sector as the profit-maximising nature of the private sector might prevent it from targeting specific demographics.
Taking the initiative to get the process started.	The most important step is taking the initiative to get the project off the ground. This can be done by the ministry linked to the SME sector or the country's central bank. This initial step might vary between countries depending on the internal mechanisms related to how projects are started. For example, some countries could decide to kick-start the ground research required to create a public sector SME rating agency if they see merit in its potential benefits. However, other countries might first require that the concept fits into its development objectives and goals. Once the concept has the necessary approvals, the next step would be securing the requisite funding and operationalising the project. Many countries have pondered on the issue of access to credit and introducing a rating service that can alleviate this; the problem is that not many governments have taken a proactive step to kick-start the process of exploring the prospects of creating such an organisation.
Incorporating a hybrid model which includes an investor pays model that credits subscribers with a certain number of rating requests per annum.	This would be an innovative approach and an alternative financial model. The traditional investor pays model involves investors paying a subscription fee to access the data of rated entities. The proposed model incorporates a similar approach but adds an additional element in which subscribers purchase a certain number of rating credits, which the public sector grading agency then executes. The model was incorporated due to the large focus on access to market and securing business opportunities. Within this model, large non-financial corporations can utilise their credits to obtain ratings on their existing or new vendors and better understand these entities' financial, operational, and technical capabilities. This approach can also be replicated with financial corporates, as they would have a large client base and could benefit from either SME credit ratings or due diligence ratings. It would ease the public sector rating agency's business development burden of securing individual SME rating mandates as this function is passed onto corporates who purchase "credit rating bundle credits". From in-depth surveys, the consensus is that these corporates (financial and non-financial) would be interested in using these subscription services, which could be a viable option. The difficult part in this process is modelling the number of rating credits within each type of subscription service, the costs of the subscription service and how to structure the overall value proposition so that it aligns with the needs of all stakeholders.

(continued)

Table 7.4 (continued)

Insights & recommendations	Further elaboration
Robust modelling of the economic and socioeconomic benefits that the public sector rating agency can bring about.	Based on the author's research and engagements with governments that have attempted to create these public sector rating agencies, the major reason these organisations were not brought to fruition is that there was no robust modelling on the potential benefits these ratings could bring about. Countries that have looked into SME credit ratings have quoted the general benefits; however, they have not attempted to forecast the potential economic or socioeconomic benefits and showcase some tangible values that could strike home with related stakeholders. Clearly outlining the potential tangible benefits is crucial as most of these projects focus exclusively on the financial and legal implications without conducting a proper cost-benefit analysis inclusive of the actual economic benefits. Incorporating these benefits allows for the associated costs and legal implications to be better contextualised, thereby enhancing decision-making outcomes.[15] It is important that a third-party firm models these potential benefits to ensure that the findings are not biassed in any way.
Extensive stakeholder events	Engaging with as many stakeholders as possible is important to build momentum around the concept and its benefits to the country. This is important as many stakeholders might be against the concept, and it is important to engage with these stakeholders and address their concerns about the project.[16] Hosting stakeholder engagement events can be a great way to engage with multiple stakeholders and to have an open discussion on the pros and cons of the organisation. The greater buy-in that the concept receives, the higher the probability that it will be brought to fruition. These engagements should occur within the pre-feasibility study, the comprehensive feasibility study, and the design phase of the organisation. Similar engagements were proven to be quite effective within the project that Credit Rating Analytics is busy with, as it has allowed stakeholders to be better informed on the concept and its potential benefits. Due to the concept being in its infancy stage, it is generally misunderstood by many stakeholders, including personnel within the traditional credit rating industry. This can then result in stakeholders not buying into the concept due to them not fully understanding it, which was the case within the project that Credit Rating Analytics is busy with. These extensive engagements are then critical and also provide a platform for stakeholders to provide their inputs into how the organisation should be structured. Catering to the needs of all stakeholders is imperative to the organisation's long-term viability, and many of these needs should be identified when the organisation is operational.

(continued)

[15] Pillay, S., Ismail, Z., Sikochi, A., & Odii, C. (2023). Introduction to Business Government and International Economy (BGIE)—New Course Development. Harvard Business School. https://www.hbs.edu/faculty/Pages/item.aspx?num=65812 (Accessed 1 June 2024).

[16] Stakeholders that are against the concept are critically important as they might provide valuable insights into why the concept might not work, and they might look at things from a different perspective. Within the feasibility study, it is extremely important to be as unbiased as possible to ensure that all the negatives around the project are considered and included in the decision-making process.

Table 7.4 (continued)

Insights & recommendations	Further elaboration
Proper research into the legal implications with a focus on empirical examples of how these legal implications have materialised in the past.	The legal implications of a public sector rating system are frequently quoted as the largest inhibiting factor that has curtailed these organisations' development. The key concerns related to these legal implications are the legal claims that could arise should false ratings be handed out. Whilst this is a legitimate concern, it is often blown out of proportion and not contextualised to the legal framework in the country or region in question.[17] To properly understand these implications, it is important to create a database of all the fines and penalties handed out to credit rating agencies and then conduct a separate analysis to determine the probabilities of these penalties and fines materialising in the country in question. Annexure one outlines how some of these legal implications could materialise, and deductions can be made to determine the likelihood of similar legal action occurring. In many instances, countries will realise that these legal implications could arise in theory, but their legal and compliance frameworks could decrease the probability of it occurring on a large-scale basis. It is also important to analyse how the public sector credit rating agencies are treated from a regulation perspective in Europe, as some have applied for and were granted regulatory exemptions. Research into the legal and compliance model in Europe should then be considered when conducting the legal feasibility, and an emphasis should be placed on the feasibility of implementing a similar compliance model.
Creating a well-experienced and strategically positioned working committee for the project.	Creating an internal working committee would be important as it will bring together a group of experts who could contribute positively to the project. The working committee will include employees from the government agency which has initiated the project, but this can be extended to external consultants who are experts on the subject matter. The committee members could be segregated into different working groups and tasked with providing important recommendations on the project's strategic direction. Within the project that Credit Rating Analytics is busy with, the working committee comprises of around 15-20 members at the director/deputy director level within the government agency. The committee was formed when the project was commissioned, and there are ongoing engagements with these committee members. All decisions within the project have to be approved by a common consensus, which allows for multiple inputs which are better aligned with the needs of SMEs. The committee should include key personnel from different divisions to consider diverging views.

[17] Annexure one provides an overview of some of the penalties, fines, and legal action that were taken against the credit rating industry. Whilst some of these penalties have been severe, there have not been many cases linked to false ratings, as the majority are linked to inconsistencies in the credit rating process, which contravened the regulatory framework in some of these countries.

Table 7.5 The ancillary services which can optimise overall outcomes

Insights and recommendations	Further elaboration
Creating an SME credit rating preparation program.	As indicated previously, there are no working examples of such a program apart from the initiative that Credit Rating Analytics is busy with, and many lessons can be learned from how effective it has been in that country. The key considerations for creating such a program are as follows: • There needs to be an incentive to get SMEs to want to enter the program and eventually get rated, as many of these businesses remain informal due to various reasons. Based on market feedback, CRA determined that it would be wise to include a basic SME due diligence rating for SMEs within the rating preparation program. This would cover KYC and a basic overview of the SME and the business owner's claims. The key takeaway is that the basic ratings would be seen as a tangible value add to these businesses before the formal SME ratings are handed out at a later stage. • The program needs to be structured so that it does not overwhelm SMEs but is instead a sequenced and palatable transition. • Extensive research is needed into the strategic benefits of the rating preparation program to the organisation and the country as a whole. The program will benefit the SME credit rating unit, play a major role in formalising the SME sector, and positively contribute to the overall economy. Other key stakeholders might then want to participate due to these broader benefits.

Part IV

Creating a Private Sector SME Credit Rating Industry Within a Country

This section includes recommendations on how to create a private sector SME credit rating industry. It should be noted that having a private or public sector industry is not mutually exclusive as both can complement each other and operate concurrently, as is the case in Europe. The question should not be which of the two to establish but rather the feasibility of creating both that cater to different market segments. Furthermore, in countries where governments are not keen on introducing a public sector model, the private sector could be a viable solution. Within this chapter, we showcase what is required to create a private sector SME credit rating industry and subsequently introduce the private sector SME credit rating ecosystem model. The private sector ecosystem model is a collective approach by various stakeholders who are all working together to achieve the common goal of access to finance. We will unpack how this innovative concept can be put into practice and showcase how it has worked in other countries.[1]

[1] We introduced the ecosystem model when we referred to the Credit Rating and Performance Scheme, which was implemented in India. We re-introduce this concept in this section and provide insights into how it can be practically implemented within any country.

8

Creating a Private Sector Credit Rating Industry

8.1 An Overview of Some of the Prominent Countries with Private SME Credit Rating Industries and How and Why these Industries were Created

The previous chapters have provided a background into the private sector SME credit rating industry and a mapping of the global SME credit rating agencies. However, it should be noted that even if private sector credit rating agencies exist within different regions, it does not imply significant SME credit rating coverage within the underlying countries.[1] There are just a handful of countries with vast SME credit rating coverage, mainly concentrated in Asia. The rationale behind the creation of these industries varies, and it is either down to a government initiative to boost access to finance or to complement a regulatory function. As indicated previously, one of the prominent countries with an SME credit rating industry is India, where the industry has evolved over the past 20 years. The industry was initially kickstarted via the Performance and Credit Rating Scheme and involved a multistakeholder approach, in which these ratings were used as an access-to-finance enabler. The regulatory approach was also a major boost to the

[1] This is owing to the shortcoming mentioned in the previous chapters and the reluctance of the private sector to provide these services on a broad-scale basis.

S. Pillay, *The Next Frontier in SME Ratings*,
https://doi.org/10.1007/978-3-031-54015-8_8

industry and gave birth to the bank loan rating product. This product now makes up the majority of ratings that are handed out to the SME sector.

The other Asian country where these ratings are widely available is Bangladesh, which is also owing to the use of these credit ratings for regulatory purposes. Within Bangladesh, seven credit rating agencies provide SME credit ratings, with the industry experiencing robust growth over recent times.[2] These ratings are vital to the country's vast and fast-growing SME sector and are used as a key regulatory tool. Apart from India and Bangladesh, the private sector industry is available in Spain, France, and Italy; however, there are not a significant number of SME credit rating agencies, and the concept is still gaining momentum. The other countries mentioned in the initial chapters host either one or just a handful of SME credit rating agencies, highlighting the developing nature of the concept in most countries.

8.2 The Technical Requirements, Market Infrastructure, and Regulatory Requirements to Set Up a Robust SME Credit Rating Industry

There are various requirements to consider when establishing an SME credit rating industry within any country. Some of these requirements are similar to those related to the public sector concept outlined in the chapter above. To avoid repetition, we will attempt to focus on some of the other specific private sector regulatory requirements. These requirements are as follows:

1. The backing of the ministry that is linked to the SME sector
2. The legal and regulatory requirements
3. Traditional credit rating agencies
4. A buy-in from the traditional and non-traditional credit providers
5. Capacity building initiatives
6. Technical expertise (if applicable)
7. A buy-in from the Central Bank

[2] These are the Credit Rating Agency of Bangladesh, Credit Rating Information & Services (CRISL), Emerging Credit Rating Ltd, Argus Credit Rating Services, Waso Credit Rating Company (BD) Ltd, The Bangladesh Rating Agency Limited (BDRAL), Emerging Credit Rating Limited (ECRL), INCRA Limited.

8.2.1 Support from the Ministry Linked to the SME Sector

Although it is not a prerequisite when creating a private sector credit rating agency, it is a major boost if the industry has significant support from the ministry linked to SME development. Capacity building and awareness are non-existent in countries where the private sector goes about it in isolation, and the ministry linked to the SME sector can be an essential strategic partner that can assist in this regard. Due to the benefits of the ratings to the broader SME ecosystem, this ministry might also proactively assist in getting buy-ins from other key stakeholders in order to increase coverage and the acceptability of these ratings. The ministry could provide a subsidy to SMEs similar to the Performance and Credit Rating Scheme in India, which played a major role in increasing the availability of these ratings. Many private sector companies take it upon themselves to introduce the concept into a country and struggle to get significant traction when there is limited or no government support. Governments are also guilty of not having much knowledge of the concept and its potential benefits; however, their intervention could be highly beneficial to its success.

8.2.2 The Legal and Regulatory Requirements

Relative to the public sector model, the underlying dynamics with the financial model of private sector credit rating agencies result in a higher propensity to hand out false credit ratings. A comprehensive regulatory framework is imperative to prevent these conflicts of interest from occurring, and this section unpacks some of the requirements to establish such a framework.[3] The success of the SME credit rating concept is directly linked to the confidence that end users have in the accuracy of these ratings. A comprehensively regulated industry then provides surety to the end users of these ratings that extensive measures are in place to ensure that there is limited room for conflicts of interest to arise. SME credit ratings are regulated using the regulatory framework applicable to traditional credit rating agencies (focusing on sovereign, corporate, and derivative ratings). In the aftermath of the global financial crisis, many countries have created or enhanced these regulatory frameworks. Regulatory frameworks exclusive to SME credit rating agencies

[3] We touched on this within the section related to establishing a public sector SME credit rating agency, within this section we unpack the legal and regulatory requirements which are applicable to a private sector industry.

are currently unavailable in almost all countries. However, the author believes a serious case should be made about creating such regulatory frameworks. The rationale behind this is that traditional credit rating frameworks do not fully address the risks linked to the SME credit rating concept, and some of the regulations might also not be applicable, resulting in elevated and unnecessary regulatory costs. Creating a distinct regulatory framework could be beneficial for the following reasons (Table 8.1).

Obtaining regulatory approval will also be a prerequisite before ratings can be handed out, and the SME credit rating function falls under the regulations pertaining to traditional rating agencies. This would be straightforward for existing credit rating agencies as they would merely need to inform the regulator of their intention to hand out SME ratings and then provide evidence of their ability to do this. For newly established SME credit rating agencies, there would be a few requirements, which are summarised in Table 8.2.

8.2.3 Traditional Credit Rating Agencies

Most SME credit rating units are sub-divisions within established credit rating agencies focusing on the traditional credit rating space. Creating a private sector SME credit rating industry would then require convincing these existing credit rating agencies to develop an SME credit rating offering. Alternatively, it would require convincing SME credit rating agencies from other jurisdictions to create a subsidiary. This is likely one of the most difficult steps as there are a handful of SME credit rating agencies in most regions (if any), so there would need to be engagements with existing credit rating agencies to convince them to create an SME rating division. Considering the profitability levels associated with the SME credit rating industry compared to the traditional rating industry, this will be no easy task. There would then need to be some sort of added incentive which could be in the form of a bespoke regulatory framework or a subsidised SME credit rating model. Egypt is an example of a country which attempted to ease the registration requirements to promote SME credit rating agencies to enter the market in 2018.[4] This approach appeared to be a good idea in principle, but few regional SME credit rating agencies could exploit this opportunity. Such regulatory

[4] Egypt wanted to attract SME credit rating agencies as they were aware of the potential benefits of these ratings and how it could align with the development of SMEs within the country. The regulators specifically mentioned that they wanted to increase the number of SME credit rating agencies and approved the licencing of such entities. More insights can be found here: Egypt Today. (2019). FRA approves licencing SMEs credit rating companies. [Online]. Egypt Today. https://www.egypttoday.com/Article/3/74402/FRA-approves-licensing-SMEs-credit-rating-companies (Accessed 5 March 2022).

Table 8.1 The benefits of a bespoke regulatory framework

Benefits	Further elaboration
1. It could result in a lower amount of conflicts of interest and run-ins with the law amongst SME credit rating agencies	Having a regulatory framework that focuses on the idiosyncratic risks associated with the SME credit rating industry would allow the regulatory body to have better oversight over these risks. For example, the reporting requirements and focus areas within these regulatory frameworks would be directly linked to the risks involved, making it easier to identify these underlying risks. The regulatory frameworks related to the traditional credit rating agencies are generally linked to risk factors that might not be relevant to the SME credit rating space, resulting in inappropriate reporting requirements and inefficient regulatory outcomes
2. It could attract an increased number of credit rating agencies or interested firms to create an SME credit rating offering	One of the major hindrances to the creation of SME credit rating agencies is the burdensome regulatory requirements related to the establishment of the agency and its ongoing upkeep. Large upfront capital requirements or high annual regulatory fees are not aligned with the profit margins associated with the SME credit industry, making it challenging to justify establishing an SME credit rating agency. The ongoing reporting requirements, which require a sophisticated in-house compliance team combined with the high annual regulatory fees in some countries, create an environment which is not conducive to profitability. For credit rating agencies wanting to focus exclusively on SME credit ratings, the initial operating years are the most difficult to endure as the business model requires scale to become profitable, and scale takes time to build up. Including high regulatory costs within these initial operating years significantly decreases the financial viability of establishing such an entity unless it is part of a larger traditional credit rating agency and can leverage off income streams from other businesses

(continued)

Table 8.1 (continued)

Benefits	Further elaboration
3. It would provide peace of mind to existing end users of these ratings and, thus, encourage higher use of these ratings	The effectiveness of the SME credit rating concept is linked to the value that end users extract from these ratings. Value is only extracted when there is confidence around the underlying accuracy of these ratings, which is heavily linked to the regulatory framework under which the industry operates. Operating under a tailored framework would provide greater comfort to the end users of these ratings and thus increase their propensity to want to include these ratings in their decision-making processes. Within previous work that was completed around this concept, a large number of financial firms indicated that stringent regulatory frameworks would be a prerequisite for including these ratings in their credit processes

frameworks need to be more targeted in that they should focus on getting traditional rating agencies to establish their SME credit rating divisions as separate entities which are governed by different sets of regulations. Explicitly stating that these divisions should operate separately and be governed by a separate set of regulations creates more clarity on the part of the rating agencies and makes it a more attractive prospect. The regulatory reporting requirements of credit rating agencies are a major internal cost and one which would be significantly increased if the rating agency stepped into the SME rating space using a traditional regulatory framework. The sheer quantum of SME ratings handed out, and the corresponding regulatory costs would be the major factor behind this, which might decrease traditional rating agencies' appetite to create these divisions. Additional incentives, such as a subsidised model, would need to be introduced concurrently to make it more appealing; we will discuss the subsidised approach within the ecosystem model in the next chapter.

Creating this conducive environment could be viewed as the first step, as the industry will only thrive if a large number of service providers are placing a concerted effort to provide these services on a country-wide basis.

Table 8.2 The requirements to establish a credit rating agency

Requirement	Further elaboration
Assembling a board of directors	This is one of the primary requirements in most jurisdictions in which the rating agencies are required to assemble a competent board of directors. There are generally specifications around the number of independent directors and their experience. This requirement varies per region and also has requirements about the number and location that these directors should be resident in. The board will play an essential role in the organisation's strategic direction and will provide technical guidance and oversight
A capital requirement	Within many jurisdictions, there are requirements related to how much capital the rating agency should hold prior to being established. These capital requirements can be high and are thus an important consideration; regulators sometimes provide concessions to these requirements, which are linked to the size of the credit rating agency and its projected turnover. These requirements are established to determine if the rating agency is adequately capitalised to carry out rating activities. It is also implemented to ensure they have sufficient funds to pay any regulatory penalties[5]

(continued)

[5] Any concessions with credit rating regulators need to be agreed upon at registration and are generally available to smaller credit rating agencies. This is done to promote new entrants to the market and to increase competition which is much needed within the credit rating space.

Table 8.2 (continued)

Requirement	Further elaboration
Fit and proper requirements of staff members	Regulators will have requirements linked to the experience and qualifications of staff of the proposed rating agency. This ensures that the ratings handed out are of the highest standard and aligned with industry norms and international standards. The fit and proper requirements are non-negotiable in most jurisdictions, and credit rating agencies are required to adhere to these requirements and recruit staff to match these specifications. As there are currently no SME credit rating regulations, there are no specific requirements linked to experience within the SME credit rating space, but rather, some experience requirements linked to the traditional rating space
An upfront licencing fee	Most credit rating applications involve a licencing fee that must be paid before the process can begin. This fee covers the government's internal costs to process the application and is generally non-refundable
Admin, registration, and other requirements	In all instances, the proposed rating agency will need to register a company within the country in which it intends to obtain a licence. There are then many administrative requirements that the rating agencies require, and these can be discussed upon initiation of the licencing process

8.2.4 A Buy-in from Traditional and Non-Traditional Credit Providers as Well as Non-Financial Firms

After obtaining a buy-in from credit rating agencies to create an SME credit rating division, the next step would be to get a buy-in from the financial sector, which provides funding to the SME sector. This is extremely important as actual SMEs will only take up these ratings if financial institutions accept them. The ideal approach to this would be if the ministry linked to the

SME sector reaches out directly to the central bank or the country's banking association. Getting a buy-in from the central bank and the banking association would translate into country-wide adoption of the ratings, increasing the demand amongst SMEs. A similar approach was initially taken in India to ensure that the majority of banks accepted the ratings. SMEs with high credit ratings were awarded preferential predetermined interest rates from participating banks, which further increased the scheme's appeal. The ideal outcome would be obtaining a country-wide buy-in; however, if this is not possible, the next best bet would be obtaining an individual buy-in from financial institutions. This would be an extensive process, and it would make sense to start with the larger banks first, as alternative banks should then come on board thereafter. The easiest way to get these financial institutions to utilise these ratings is by showcasing the credit-scoring capabilities of the rating agencies, their industry-specific methodologies, and the default and transition statistics within the larger sector that they currently cover.

It is also important to obtain a buy-in from non-financial firms which can procure from SMEs. The SME rating concept, as previously discussed, can be effective at securing business opportunities due to its ability to reduce the information asymmetry between contracting parties. A substantial number of these large enterprises want to procure from SMEs but might not have the time to conduct the requisite due diligence on these businesses. Many of these businesses currently struggle with quality due diligence reports and would subscribe to a service which caters to this need. This could also be an indirect tool to get SMEs to want to get rated, as it could expose them to business opportunities with large corporates that already accept these ratings.

8.2.5 Capacity Building Initiatives

Capacity building is required at various stages when introducing the concept; this can be segregated as follows:

- *Prior to the concept being introduced into a country:*
  This is important and involves capacity-building initiatives with related multilateral organisations or experts in this field who would upskill the government on the concept. Creating an entire SME credit rating industry is no easy task, and most governments would be unfamiliar with the concept. The capacity-building would revolve around introductions to SME ratings, its effectiveness, and case studies on countries that have successfully created similar industries.

- *When there are plans to introduce the concept into a country:*
  This will occur within the feasibility study stage and involve all of the key stakeholders and users of these ratings. These stakeholders will be upskilled on how the concept could add value to their respective industries or public sector divisions. Within the feasibility study phase, these stakeholders will be probed as to whether the industry should be set up or not, and capacity-building will thus be required to bring them up to speed on the concept. Capacity building could be done via stakeholder engagement events, which would provide a brief overview of the concept and its effectiveness. The optimal time to do this would be after the internal pre-feasibility phase and prior to the comprehensive feasibility study within which these stakeholders would participate.
- *Within the design phase of the organisation:*
  This would involve much more complex capacity-building efforts with these stakeholders as discussions will revolve around the potential creation of an ecosystem model or multistakeholder collaborations. The capacity-building efforts here will involve presenting in-depth data and findings from the feasibility study around how, why, when, and by whom the concept can be introduced into the country. Within the multistakeholder approach, each stakeholder has a specific role; these stakeholders will then need to be upskilled in these roles and the concept before getting a buy-in from them.
- *When the industry is being introduced:*
  This will involve capacity-building initiatives with stakeholders that would be directly involved in this industry, which would include but not limited to:

  - The staff of the grading agency.
  - Internal stakeholders within the government that will be involved in the industry.
  - Regulators that will be overseeing the SME credit rating function (most regulators are not too familiar with these ratings).
  - The staff within financial institutions that will be end users of these ratings.
  - Actual SMEs, to build up demand for these ratings.

- *Post the establishment of the industry:*
  This is an important portion of the capacity-building initiative and will involve continuous engagements with SMEs to ensure that they are aware of the concept. A common issue in most countries where these services are available is that even if the rating agencies provide a compelling value

proposition, there is still limited usage of the concept due to limited awareness of these ratings. For the industry to thrive in any particular country, there will need to be constant capacity-building and marketing initiatives around the concept. The capacity-building initiatives should be extended to key stakeholders that are directly linked to SMEs in an advisory capacity. This will include professional services firms such as lawyers, accountants, business consultants, bank intermediaries, and similar organisations. These firms are the go-to advisory source for SMEs, and having them upskilled on the concept would be important as they could then expand upon the SME credit rating concept whenever there are discussions around access to finance.

The capacity-building requirement is thus quite essential and should be an ongoing initiative from the project's onset. A vital consideration post-implementation is to conduct research assignments that measure these ratings' effectiveness. These findings, if in the affirmative, can then be used to demonstrate the efficacy of these ratings and thereby boost demand. Reference should also be made to other studies with empirical evidence of the benefits of these ratings, such as those put forward within chapter four of this report.

8.2.6 Technical Expertise (If Applicable)

In this context, we would refer to technical expertise at an SME credit rating level. As this is lacking in most regions due to the infancy stage of the industry, it might be difficult for the rating agencies to create these divisions and attract human capital with the requisite experience in this subject area. An industry norm is, however, to enter into technical agreements with other credit rating agencies in different jurisdictions. This would then allow for knowledge sharing on the concept, which would be necessary for the sake of making improvements to the organisation. The technical sharing agreements could cover areas such as methodology development, operational procedures, systems, and research and development. The issue of a lack of adequately experienced employees could be mitigated by employing staff from related industries, such as credit teams within banks and then upskilling them on the concept. The underlying concepts underpinning the SME credit rating industry should be easy for financial and risk professionals to grasp. Capacity building and training can initially be done within the technical agreements with other rating agencies and eventually be completed internally once the rating agency is adequately skilled.

8.2.7 A Buy-in from the Central Bank

Due to the nature of these ratings and their effect on financial stability within the banking system, the ratings must have the central bank's full approval and backing. Furthermore, attaining buy-in from the central bank will improve the chances of obtaining a country-wide adoption of these ratings with banks in the country. The support of a central bank also increases the perceived credibility of these ratings, which will assist when trying to get SMEs to buy into the concept. Central banks that incorporate and promote the standardised approach to risk assessment could benefit from SME credit ratings at a firm level as this increases the level of transparency related to the underlying credit quality within SME loan portfolios. The rating agencies can then work with the central bank to create rating products which accurately capture the probability of default using a globally accepted 20-point rating scale. This could significantly increase the demand for these ratings as banks would request that SMEs with large credit exposures be rated. India's bank loan rating product was created to capture these credit exposures and has been effective at providing a much-needed regulatory service.

8.3 Examples of Countries in which the Concept has Failed and Reasons as to Why this is the Case

It is crucial to highlight the unsuccessful attempts to establish an SME credit rating industry, as these examples provide valuable insights into the factors that hindered its development. This analysis can serve as a reference point for countries aiming to establish their own industry. For instance, in Indonesia, a reputable rating agency launched a private sector SME rating agency, which initially appeared promising given the large number of SMEs and the significant credit gap. However, the initiative faced unexpectedly low demand. Despite the potential, the organisation struggled to rate a substantial number of SMEs. Based on the author's observations, the failure can be attributed to several key factors (Table 8.3).

The shortcomings of the approach taken above can be an excellent example of what to avoid when trying to establish a private sector credit rating industry. The critical takeaway is that it is difficult for an individual firm to take it upon themselves to create an SME credit rating industry, and there definitely needs to be government involvement and a multistakeholder approach. This is particularly true for a new concept, as stakeholder needs

Table 8.3 The reasons why SME credit ratings failed in Indonesia

Reason	Further elaboration
There was a lack of awareness and culture around utilising these ratings	Introducing these ratings into a country with little knowledge of the concept or culture of using these ratings is quite difficult. To overcome this, there needs to be significant capacity-building on the concept and ample time for it to develop. This requires patience and a long-term approach, which might entail initial loss-making years for the rating agency. Within the Indonesian example, there was no culture of using these ratings, and there wasn't a concerted capacity-building effort to adjust this. This then resulted in SMEs not being aware of the ratings and their associated benefits, which negatively affected demand
A unique financial system and borrowing structure within the SME space	The financial system applicable to the SME sector operates differently from financial systems in other jurisdictions and includes a unique borrowing structure. For example, the country has community-based lending schemes which operate on a day-to-day re-payment program for unsecured loans.[6] With SMEs obtaining credit from these channels and via other microfinance institutions, it becomes difficult to position SME credit ratings within this system without creating a bespoke offering. The SME credit ratings were not fine-tuned to cater to the unique lending approach, resulting in inefficient outcomes and limited demand
Limited investment into the SME credit rating division	The credit rating agency that provided these ratings was a traditional credit rating agency, which was quite successful in the traditional credit rating space. Profitability levels were robust within these traditional channels, and the SME credit rating space was viewed as an additional income stream. The issue that arose was the low levels of profitability within the SME space and the reluctance of the rating agency to invest heavily in this venture. The human capital contingency allocated to this newly formed division was quite small and insufficient to facilitate the required scale that would lead to profitability. The rating agency in question likely did not see merit in allocating resources to the SME space when the return on investment was much higher within the traditional credit rating industry

(continued)

[6] KPMG. (2014). New Indonesian "Branchless Banking" and Microfinance Laws—A catalyst for micro. [Online]. KPMG. https://assets.kpmg.com/content/dam/kpmg/pdf/2016/07/id-ksa-financial-inclusion-indonesia.pdf (Accessed 10 December 2023).

Table 8.3 (continued)

Reason	Further elaboration
There was no significant buy-in from the banking system, the country's central bank, or the ministry linked to the SME sector	As indicated in the section above, this is important and was not prevalent in this scenario. There was then no industry-wide buy-in from the banks, resulting in lacklustre demand from SMEs There was also no support from the ministry linked to the SME sector, resulting in no capacity-building efforts or awareness campaigns designed to increase demand for these ratings. A subsidy scheme similar to the Indian example could have been a more appropriate option to get the concept going, but this was not available
The ratings were available for a limited time in Indonesia	The rating agency in question had these services available for 1–2 years before deciding to pull the plug. Whilst this might be viewed as a proactive approach to a loss-making initiative, it can also be viewed as an impatient approach by the rating agency. An operation running for 1–2 years without significant investment, innovation, or alignment to the needs of SMEs will inevitably result in a negative outcome. When looked at from this perspective, the entity was bound to fail due to the approach taken

must be considered before any concept can achieve widespread adoption. The next section is important in providing recommendations on how the concept can be structured to best serve related stakeholders' needs.

8.4 Recommendations on How Existing SME Credit Rating Industries can be Best Structured to Serve the Needs of Related Stakeholders

This is an integral section of the book as it includes recommendations on how the SME credit rating concept can be positioned to best serve its stakeholders' needs. The recommendations provided below are based on engagements with multiple stakeholders that have been involved in or benefited from these ratings. These stakeholders have a firsthand understanding of the perceived shortcomings of SME credit rating systems and, therefore, provide some valuable insights. When looking at stakeholder needs, it is essential to first look at the needs of individual SMEs as they form the core of the entire value proposition and the reason why the concept was created in the first instance. Some of the concepts put forward here are related to the private sector industry but can be adopted if the public sector model is implemented. These needs are as follows:

8.4.1 The Borrowing Needs of SMEs

The borrowing needs of SMEs are the primary reason why the industry was created, and it is relevant in the current economic environment due to the significant credit gap facing this sector. Although this is the basis behind the industry, it can be argued that there has not been much thought into how to best cater for the borrowing needs of SMEs when we look at the value proposition of SME credit rating agencies. The author believes that the SME credit rating industry is too much of a replication of the traditional credit rating industry in which there is no emphasis on how the rated entity raises capital. Whilst this is correct and simultaneously allows for independence in the rating process, it results in unfavourable outcomes when we attempt to replicate this model within the SME credit rating industry. This is due to the following reasons (Table 8.4).

Getting entrenched in the lending process is then vitally important to the viability and sustainability of the SME credit rating concept. How to go about doing this should be at the core of discussions when attempting to create or improve an existing credit rating division.

Apart from the borrowing needs of SMEs, providing them with critical feedback on their existing operational and financial standing is also important, as many SMEs are not too familiar with their levels of relative performance. Such feedback would showcase to SMEs where they fall short; this is important as it serves as an independent opinion on what needs improvement. SME credit rating agencies should then design their value propositions so that they can relay such feedback in an impactful manner. Individual metric rankings would be essential and should include insights into the industry averages for important metrics within the rating methodology. Providing such information within the actual SME report in an easily digestible manner would serve as a vital feedback mechanism to relay these shortcomings and to then track the progress of alleviating these issues within the ongoing surveillance phase. A large number of SMEs might not have an idea of their core weaknesses relative to other SMEs, and uncovering this can propel them to new heights. One of the objectives of the government-backed scheme in India was to do this precisely, and some of the surveys completed indicated that the scheme had achieved this mandate.[7]

[7] We unpacked these benefits in Chapter Four and further insights can be found here: NSIC. (2012). Study of the "Performance & Credit Rating Scheme for Micro & Small Enterprises". [Online]. https://www.nsic.co.in/. https://www.nsic.co.in/pdfs/STUDY/srcr2012.pdf (Accessed 3 June 2023).

Table 8.4 The reasoning behind intervening in the borrowing process

Reasoning	Further elaboration
The model used for large enterprises assumes that the borrowing needs of these businesses are taken care of by other stakeholders	When large listed or unlisted businesses approach a credit rating agency, two basic needs need to be addressed: the first and primary need is to raise capital, and the second is to obtain an independent credit rating. At the end of the process, both of these needs are taken care of as the organisation will have a corporate or investment banking team to source the best possible borrowing terms that the credit rating will enable. The problem with uniformly replicating this operating model to the SME space is that SMEs have these exact two requirements, but only the credit rating need is actively satisfied. Using the replicated model, the SME would receive the SME credit rating, but its borrowing need might not be satisfied as there is no dedicated team of experts trying to secure funding opportunities. SMEs are generally single-banked and would take the credit rating to their financial institution, which would either accept or reject the borrowing request. In this scenario, the rated entity might view the credit rating as being ineffective as it has not enabled the rated entity to fulfil its borrowing requirement. The rated entity might then cancel the credit rating mandate and not proceed with the second-year surveillance. To increase the value add of the rating process, there needs to be either a direct or indirect intervention in the lending process whilst maintaining a level of independence. This can be in the form of linking rated entities with borrowers/investors and engaging with stakeholders to determine the credibility of the rated entity, as well as providing additional insights into the SME credit rating process. Engaging with investors is a common practice within the traditional credit rating space as investor events are frequently held, and discussions are held around the credit rating quality of popular rated sectors of the economy. This is taken a step further within the sovereign space, where discussions are held about the credibility of individual sovereign or sub-sovereign entities. These engagements further decrease the information asymmetry and, depending on the credit trajectory, can increase the willingness to lend or do business with rated SMEs. As this is an industry norm, there should be similar engagements within the SME space, which could further increase the effectiveness of these ratings

(continued)

Table 8.4 (continued)

Reasoning	Further elaboration
It can increase the fee income earned by SME credit rating agencies or units	The tenuous levels of fee income associated with the SME credit rating space are one of the primary reasons why the industry has failed to develop in many countries. However, the root cause of this is the unwillingness of SMEs to pay for these ratings due to the perceived value add of the concept. Traditional credit rating agencies earn revenues which are linked to the amount of capital being raised; these fees are capped/reduced for large issuances but are still quite lucrative. One of the problems with the SME credit rating model is that it attempts to replicate the operational model utilised when rating large enterprises but fails to mimic the fee-income model. For example, within the SME credit rating space, SMEs are charged a flat rating fee which is linked to the size of their operation, and there is no fee linked to the quantum of capital being raised. Adopting this approach significantly reduces profitability and increases the required scale that is required to remain sustainable. It should be noted that SMEs would be reluctant to pay this even if SME credit rating agencies attempted to charge a basis point fee linked to the quantum of capital being raised. This would be owing to the fact that SMEs might not see the value add of the services provided to justify paying a success fee. This might be true to some extent but could be mitigated if the rating agencies attempted to involve themselves to a larger extent within the lending process. If this was done using the methods described above, SMEs might see more value in the rating process and be willing to part ways with a portion of the capital being raised. A similar model exists in many countries where intermediaries professionally put together credit applications and then attempt to source funding opportunities. These intermediaries sometimes charge a flat fee to put the credit application together and also charge a success fee based on the capital that is raised. SMEs in this scenario are open to parting ways with a portion of the capital raise as they see value in the service being rendered. SME credit rating agencies could achieve these outcomes if they were to adopt a similar model but would need to simultaneously maintain their level of independence when doing so

9

An Introduction to the SME Ecosystem Model Approach

9.1 What is an SME Credit Rating Ecosystem, and What are the Associated Benefits?

An SME credit rating ecosystem is a collaboration between various stakeholders with a vested interest in the SME space. This ecosystem model attempts to align the interests of these stakeholders so that optimal outcomes can be achieved, thus proliferating the development of this important sector. As indicated in the previous chapters, the private sector credit rating model operating in isolation cannot achieve profitable and sustainable outcomes. This is due to many factors; however, the overall outcomes are optimised when the concept is incorporated into a multistakeholder approach. The ecosystem model has no specific format or structure as it is a fairly new concept, and the structure might vary between countries. India set a precedent for such a model with the Performance and Credit Rating Scheme, which proved effective over the duration it was in place. Some of the benefits of the government-backed scheme were highlighted in four separate surveys, and the findings from the last survey were highlighted in chapter four. Additional insights into the benefits of adopting the ecosystem model are explored below:

S. Pillay, *The Next Frontier in SME Ratings*,
https://doi.org/10.1007/978-3-031-54015-8_9

9.1.1 The Ecosystem Model can Achieve Optimal Outcomes in the Access to Finance Space

The ecosystem model includes key stakeholders from the financial industry, which buy into the SME rating concept at the onset and provide preferential borrowing rates depending on the credit rating given. Financial institutions are among the most important stakeholders in the ecosystem as they are the largest end users of these ratings and ultimately determine their effectiveness. Their participation within the ecosystem model is then imperative; within the Indian example, these financial institutions, via the banker's association, collectively agreed to include these credit ratings into their credit-scoring processes. Furthermore, these entities also agreed to provide preferential borrowing rates to SMEs that achieved and maintained elevated credit ratings.[1] Based on observations from the Indian model, obtaining buy-in from the bankers' association and the country's central bank is imperative. If this can be achieved, getting the concept off the ground is made much easier as the ratings will be widely accepted, increasing the demand for these ratings amongst SMEs.

9.1.2 It Ensures that the Concept Remains Much More Profitable for SME Credit Rating Agencies

As explained within the sections above, the SME credit rating concept remains unprofitable in most instances as SMEs are quite sensitive from a pricing perspective and are not very open to parting ways with their hard-earned revenue.[2] It then becomes difficult to price these ratings competitively, resulting in the industry requiring substantial scale to achieve some level of profitability. A key feature of the ecosystem model is the government grants which are handed out to SMEs to obtain these ratings. These government grants increase the appetite of SMEs to obtain these ratings as the government pays a portion of the rating fee. Within the Indian model, the government grant was a key enabler to the overall success of the ecosystem model, as evidenced by the fact that the industry partially collapsed after it was retracted. The government grant mechanism was one of the primary reasons

[1] Ministry of Micro, Small and Medium Enterprises. (2015). Performance and Credit Rating Scheme for Micro & Small Enterprises. [Online]. Ministry of Micro, Small and Medium Enterprises. https://msme.gov.in/sites/default/files/PCR_EN.pdf (Accessed 01 June 2023).

[2] Asking SMEs to part ways with their hard-earned capital for a concept that does not provide a guaranteed outcome can be difficult; this often results in SMEs attempting to negotiate the rating fee which further compresses the already small income that would be derived.

why a large number of rating agencies decided to enter the SME credit rating space, and it can thus be used as an effective tool to attract credit rating agencies. When the scheme was first launched in India, it was meant to be rolled out by the Small and Medium Enterprise Rating Agency (SMERA); however, all of the existing credit rating agencies in the country had also requested to be included. Introducing the concept within any country via the ecosystem model and appropriate regulations could then be a great way to attract international SME rating agencies to enter the market. This is needed as there is a global scarcity of SME credit rating agencies, and even if a country wants to create an SME credit rating industry, there might be no local or even regional SME credit rating agencies. A grant system could be a viable solution to overcome this and increase the industry's overall sustainability.

9.1.3 It Speeds Up the Culture Behind Using these Ratings and Increases Demand from SMEs for these Ratings

As the SME credit rating concept is fairly new in most jurisdictions, there is limited culture around using these ratings. Limited culture is due to a lack of awareness of the concept and its associated benefits. Furthermore, SMEs might not be willing to try out a concept that does not have a guaranteed outcome; however, if the majority of the rating fee is subsidised, they might have a higher propensity to take up these ratings. With the culture for using these ratings being non-existent in most markets, the ecosystem model could then be a great way to increase the awareness around these ratings.

9.1.4 The Ecosystem Model could be an Important Mechanism to Address Underlying Issues Linked to the SME Sector, such as Access to Finance and Access to Market

As indicated in the previous chapters, improvements in access to finance and access to market are a major area of focus for many governments and multilateral organisations throughout the world. With the SME credit rating concept proven to be effective at improving these concepts, the ecosystem model could be a viable solution for governments that want to target these issues. This can be used as the substantiated evidence needed to get a buy-in for the grant system, which would be required to kick-start the concept.

9.1.5 Recommendations on How to Create an SME Credit Rating Ecosystem and Examples of SME Credit Rating Ecosystems in Practice

Creating an SME credit rating ecosystem model involves a multistakeholder approach in which all stakeholders are working towards a common goal. This is a multistep model and can be summarised within the infographic below (Fig. 9.1).

As per the infographic above, the first step involves conceptualising the idea and then initiating its creation. The ministry mandated to oversee the SME industry would take the lead on this and kick-start the process of establishing an SME credit rating industry.[3] Multilateral organisations with knowledge of the concept could assist with awareness campaigns with various governments as the concept remains quite opaque and unknown in many jurisdictions.[4] The ministry linked to the SME sector would then conduct a pre-feasibility and comprehensive feasibility study to determine the viability of introducing the SME credit rating concept into the country and doing so via the SME credit rating ecosystem model. If deemed feasible, the ministry linked to the SME sector would initially reach out to various stakeholders

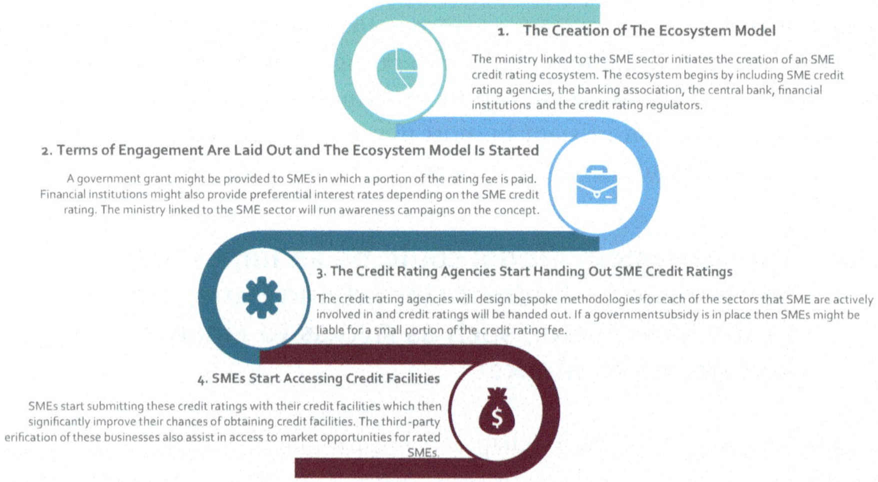

Fig. 9.1 The multistep approach to the eco-system model

[3] The country's central bank could also take the initiative to do so as it would have a mandate of promoting SME development and has taken the lead on the concept of SME credit ratings in other countries.

[4] This would follow a similar approach to that which was put forward within the chapter related to how to go about creating a public sector credit rating agency.

and indicate their intent to promote the concept via the ecosystem approach; this could be done via a round table event. Once stakeholders are on board, agreements can be reached regarding the role of each stakeholder within the ecosystem and the terms of engagement. The terms of engagement would include:

- Details on the government subsidy/grant that would be provided,
- The use of these ratings by financial institutions and,
- The required specifications of the ratings and turnaround times.

Implementing such a model would be done on a broad-scale basis, and credit rating agencies would need to enter into service-level agreements and abide by predetermined turnaround times so that the ratings do not stall the overall credit decision process. The regulators would also need to be briefed, and they will play a major role in this process as they ultimately regulate the SME credit rating function in the country. They would need to approve the underlying technical dynamics of the model to ensure that it does not infringe on the quality and accuracy of these ratings. Once it has received regulatory approval, formal agreements can be signed by parties involved in the ecosystem model. The SME credit rating ecosystem would then be open for business, and credit ratings would be handed out. Due to the scale at which ratings would be handed out, credit rating agencies would need to strategize on a country-wide rollout.

A major focus post-establishment should be on awareness campaigns to promote these ratings. This is imperative as the concept remains unknown in most countries, and its usage would be directly linked to awareness amongst individual SMEs and other key stakeholders. Based on previous projects that the author has completed on this subject area, a lack of awareness is one of the key shortcomings inhibiting the industry's development. In countries where financial institutions widely accept the ratings, and there are strong value propositions from the rating agencies, take-up is still tenuous as SMEs are unaware of both the concept and its benefits. Awareness campaigns must be geared not only towards individual SMEs but also to key centres of influence that are linked to the SME industry. As aforementioned in previous chapters, these key centres of influence are professional service firms held in high regard by SMEs and are the go-to advisory source. The ideal way to bring these professional service firms on board is via industry representative bodies at a national level. This would be an efficient approach as it will ensure that a larger number of professionals are targeted within such awareness campaigns rather than individually approaching these professionals.

Rolling out a government grant is essential in countries with no culture of using these ratings. It is also difficult to attract credit rating agencies to create SME credit rating divisions or even attract new players to the market. A government subsidy changes the appeal of wanting to create an SME credit rating unit and can be an effective tool if structured correctly. The recommendations for creating a government subsidy are as follows (Table 9.1).

Table 9.1 Recommendation when creating a government subsidy scheme

Recommendation	Further elaboration
Creating a staggered subsidy structure	A staggered subsidy structure will involve providing a subsidy that varies based on the company's size. Taking this approach will ensure that the credit rating agencies earn a fee which is related to the level of effort put into the rating and will allow them to price their services accordingly. This is important as the level of effort associated with rating a medium-sized company is much higher than rating a microenterprise. Credit rating agencies already utilise this approach in some jurisdictions, so it will complement their fee structures well
Providing a specific development subsidy to credit rating agencies	A development subsidy is important as it ensures that the rating agencies have adequate resources to properly develop their internal systems so that the SMEs can be rated in the most efficient way possible. These research and development subsidies could ensure that the required technological advancements are included in the rating process. Technological improvements generally reduce the amount of human intervention required, increase profitability, and expedite the time required to complete an SME credit rating
	The problem with introducing subsidised rating fees is that it might reduce the desire to innovate, as the industry might become accustomed to always being profitable due to the subsidy being in place. This can be viewed as the downfall of the Indian subsidy scheme, as almost all of the rating agencies struggled to maintain profitability after the subsidy scheme was retracted. Had these rating agencies invested heavily in technology to automate the credit rating process and optimise methodology development, their profitability profile would have significantly changed and ensured that their SME credit rating units remained in business. The research and development subsidy should then be an important tool to ensure that the industry remains sustainable over the long run

(continued)

(continued)

Recommendation	Further elaboration
Robust oversight	Incorporating a subsidy-backed scheme could greatly boost the industry but could result in significant conflicts of interest due to the number of ratings being handed out. These conflicts of interest could jeopardise the perceived accuracy of these ratings and result in inefficient outcomes for all stakeholders. There then needs to be robust oversight over and above that provided by regulators to ensure that these potential conflicts of interest are kept at a minimum. This could be in the form of regular audits by the ministry providing the subsidy or even via direct engagements with rated entities. The subsidised ratings could also lead to fraudulent activities and significant leverage being given to SMEs (as they would need to agree to be rated), which could result in negative outcomes
Retracting the subsidy in a gradual manner	Introducing a subsidised scheme is important to the industry's overall development; however, the manner in which the subsidy scheme is retracted is equally important. Retracting the scheme in an abrupt manner could shock the industry as there would not be a sufficient period to allow the rating agencies to adjust to an environment in which there are no subsidies in place. The recommendation would then be to gradually retract the subsidy to ensure that it provides the rating agencies sufficient time to transition to the lower subsidised rating fees. Gradually reducing the subsidy allows the government and rating agencies to observe the market demand for lower subsidised fees. This will allow for strategies to be developed that can compensate for the lower subsidised fee and thus improve the long-term sustainability of these entities
Ongoing research and field engagements on the effectiveness of the subsidy and ecosystem model	Ongoing research into the effectiveness of the subsidised scheme is important to ensure that the overall ecosystem model is operating efficiently. Positive feedback received from surveying rated SMEs could also effectively showcase the potential benefits of these ratings and thus increase demand amongst unrated SMEs. These findings could add value after the subsidy scheme is retracted as they showcase the potential benefits of these ratings and, therefore, serve as a means to maintain demand in a post-subsidised period

(continued)

(continued)

Recommendation	Further elaboration
Learning from India	Countries wanting to implement a subsidised scheme should properly analyse the Indian scheme as there can be a lot of lessons learnt about what worked and what did not work. As it was the first of its kind in the world, there were obviously many areas in which it could be improved and many positives regarding its effectiveness. Engagements can be done with the Ministry that oversaw the process, the country's central bank, and the individual SME rating agencies which handed out these ratings

As per the table, it is important to properly structure the grant system to ensure that it achieves maximum effectiveness and simultaneously promotes the industry's long-term sustainability. Moreover, an important component within the ecosystem model is how it is structured with financial institutions and their acceptance and use of these ratings. Financial institutions are the primary end users of these ratings, and the ecosystem model needs to be designed to cater to their needs and to ensure that these institutions broadly adopt these ratings. Further recommendations are as follows (Table 9.2).

Once these service-level agreements have been clearly defined and there is a buy-in from the respective financial institutions, it should be easy to market these ratings to actual SMEs and get a buy-in from them to use these ratings. This model is not exclusive to the private sector, as a public sector rating agency could be substituted into the ecosystem model and align itself to other stakeholders in the same way that private sector rating agencies would.[5] In such a model, the public sector rating agency would hand out all of the SME cred ratings in the manner discussed in the previous chapters. SMEs could still be provided with preferential borrowing rates in line with their ratings, and the ratings would be widely accepted. There is no default choice as to which of the two models would be best suited; however, both models should be included in a feasibility study to determine which will be best suited to the country in question.[6] It is also worth noting that there could be a combination of models within the ecosystem model, as nothing stops ratings from being handed out by both the public and private sectors.

[5] Within the public sector ecosystem model, the government grant could be in the form of a reduced rating fee, which would technically serve as an indirect subsidy.

[6] Countries would have contrasting needs, and public opinion would also be key; in some jurisdictions, the public might have little faith in the public sector's ability to provide such a service, and this would be a key consideration when determining how to introduce the concept.

Table 9.2 Recommendations for how to position these ratings to financial institutions

Recommendations	Further elaboration
Preferential borrowing terms linked to the underlying ratings	Preferential borrowing terms would be a great way to increase demand for these ratings and simultaneously provide an incentive to rated SMEs to want to improve their ratings. The important consideration here is that many banks would need to provide these preferential rates for the scheme to be effective. The preferential borrowing terms could be in the form of reduced interest rates, favourable borrowing tenures, or access to specific/bespoke lending products. These preferential borrowing terms could be a significant value add for SMEs that want to borrow and even more beneficial to SMEs with large credit facilities
A uniform credit rating scale	A uniform credit rating scale would be a must to ensure that the ratings are easily comparable across rating agencies. An example of why this is important can be observed in the current ESG rating industry, where rating agencies utilise different rating scales, making relative comparisons difficult. A uniform SME credit rating scale is then important, and this can be constructed by the regulator or in consultation with international SME credit rating agencies and related stakeholders. This would also make it easier to get a buy-in from a large number of banks as they would view the ratings as being uniform, which would easily integrate into their systems. Uniform ratings make the process much easier for individual SMEs as they can compare their performance relative to other SMEs

(continued)

Table 9.2 (continued)

Recommendations	Further elaboration
A mandatory backend system which has access to these ratings	One of the typical requirements from end users of these ratings is an easily accessible platform from which the ratings can be viewed and analysed. Some regulators make it mandatory that these ratings are publicly available, and some do not; however, for the purpose of getting a buy-in from financial institutions, the rating reports must be easily available. It is also recommended that a platform be developed that allows end users to log in and access the ratings. If a subscription fee is charged, end users can log in and model completed ratings to forecast how the rating might change under different circumstances. Such a platform could create an additional recurring income stream, adding to the SME credit rating agencies' long-term sustainability
Industry-wide service-level agreements related to turnaround times	One of the hesitancies associated with using these ratings is linked to the time taken to complete these ratings. Financial institutions are generally highly target-driven and would naturally avoid any additional services which would delay the sales process. Although SME credit ratings might be quite important to the overall credit process, financial institutions might become reluctant to utilise them if obtaining a rating does not happen timeously. There then needs to be clearly mapped out service-level agreements with turnaround times, which should be adhered to. Credit rating agencies could alter the operating model to ensure that it fits the turnaround times proposed by financial institutions

In conclusion, the ecosystem model could be an effective way to launch an SME credit rating industry within any country. Doing so without an ecosystem model has proven to be an uphill task, resulting in inefficient outcomes and limited growth for the individual SME rating agencies that have attempted to do this.

Concluding Remarks

In conclusion, the SME credit rating concept has proven to be exceptionally effective in enhancing funding and business opportunities, thereby significantly improving overall economic output and addressing socioeconomic imbalances. These ratings provide a critical assessment of SMEs, enabling better risk evaluation and fostering confidence among investors and financial institutions. However, despite their evident impact, the availability of SME credit rating services remains limited, which highlights the urgent need for strategic interventions to expand their reach, effectiveness, and acceptance. Throughout this book, we have explored various aspects of the SME credit rating concept, including its development, benefits, and implementation strategies. The concepts presented offer valuable insights and practical guidance for governments and policymakers interested in introducing or enhancing SME credit rating systems within their countries. The public sector model, which has shown positive results in Europe, stands out as a particularly effective approach. This model can serve as an exemplary framework for other nations, especially those in emerging markets, to emulate and adapt according to their specific needs and contexts.

The author's extensive interactions with governments throughout the world reveal a growing recognition of the importance of SME credit ratings. There is significant interest in establishing either public sector SME credit rating agencies or fostering private sector SME credit rating industries. Such initiatives are crucial in bridging the dire and perennial credit gap that exists in both developed and developing economies. This gap underscores the necessity for comprehensive credit rating services that can facilitate better access to financial resources and market opportunities for SMEs. The COVID-19

S. Pillay, *The Next Frontier in SME Ratings*,
https://doi.org/10.1007/978-3-031-54015-8

pandemic has further accentuated the vulnerabilities within the SME sector, making it imperative to explore innovative solutions to the funding challenges faced by these enterprises. SME credit ratings can play a pivotal role in this regard by enhancing transparency, reducing underlying information asymmetries, and fostering a more inclusive financial ecosystem. By providing a reliable assessment of creditworthiness, these ratings help SMEs secure better financing terms, lower interest rates, and longer borrowing tenures, which are essential for their growth and sustainability.

Moreover, the book delves into the public sector SME credit rating model, which has garnered considerable attention in the aftermath of the global financial crisis. This model's success in Europe demonstrates its potential to significantly improve access to finance within the SME sector. The insights gained from the author's consulting firm, Credit Rating Analytics, particularly their work on creating the world's largest public sector SME grading agency provide a practical roadmap for other countries to follow. The book also discusses the complementary nature of public and private sector SME credit rating industries. It is not a question of choosing one over the other; instead, both sectors can coexist and support each other to cater to different market segments. For countries where governments may be reluctant to introduce a public sector model, the private sector can offer a viable alternative. The private sector ecosystem model, which involves a collective effort by various stakeholders, is presented as an innovative approach to promoting SME credit ratings and improving access to finance. Ultimately, the primary intention behind writing this book is to increase awareness and availability of SME credit ratings. By doing so, we aim to address the critical challenges facing this crucial sector of the economy. The insights and recommendations provided are intended to serve as a valuable resource for policymakers, financial institutions, and other stakeholders committed to fostering a more inclusive and robust financial system for SMEs. It is hoped that this book will contribute to a greater understanding and appreciation of the SME credit rating concept, paving the way for its widespread adoption and, consequently, a more dynamic and resilient global economy.

Annexure 1: A List of Some of the Regulatory Penalties which have been Handed Out to Credit Rating Agencies Across the World

The incident/case	A further description	The repercussions and key findings
S&P Global vs ESMA (2023)	S&P Global Ratings were deemed to publish a number of credit ratings before the relevant securities had been issued (Jones, 2023)	S&P was fined 1,1 million Euros
The Securities and Exchange Commission (USA) Vs S&P Global Ratings (2022)	The rating agency was charged with violating a conflict of interest rule designed to separate credit ratings and analysts from sales and marketing efforts (SEC, 2022)	The SEC imposed a fine of $2,500,000

(continued)

S. Pillay, *The Next Frontier in SME Ratings*,
https://doi.org/10.1007/978-3-031-54015-8

(continued)

The incident/case	A further description	The repercussions and key findings
The European Securities and Markets Authority (ESMA) Vs Moody's (2021)	The breaches of the Credit Rating Agencies Regulation (CRAR) pertained to independence and the avoidance of conflicts of interest with shareholders. The breaches included: • The issuance of credit ratings in violation of the ban on issuing new ratings on entities where a credit rating agency (CRA) shareholder exceeds the 10% ownership threshold and/or is a board member of the rated entity • Failure to disclose conflicts of interest related to the 5% ownership threshold and, • Inadequate internal policies and procedures to manage shareholder conflicts of interest (ESMA, 2021)	All the breaches were found to have resulted from negligence on the part of Moody's, and ESMA fined Moody's €3,700,000
The China Securities Regulatory Commission vs Golden Credit Rating (2020)	A former executive was accused of accepting bribes to provide favourable ratings (Financial Times, 2020)	The rating agency was suspended, and direct action was taken against the agency's general manager
The Securities and Exchange Commission (USA) Vs Morningstar Ratings (2020)	The rating agency was charged with violating a conflict of interest rule designed to separate credit ratings and analysts from sales and marketing efforts (SEC, 2020)	A fine was imposed, and Morningstar has agreed to pay $3.5 million to settle the charges

(continued)

(continued)

The incident/case	A further description	The repercussions and key findings
The Securities and Exchange Commission (USA) vs Kroll Bond Rating Agency (2020)	This was in relation to civil charges that some of its practices were inadequate to ensure its ratings would be accurate (Reuters, 2020)	The SEC imposed a fine of $2,010,000
The China Securities Regulatory Commission vs Dagong (2019)	The securities regulator discovered conflicts of interest, lack of quality control, and failure to track corporate performance (SCMP, 2019)	The rating agency was taken under the control of the government for a protracted period to enable it to be reformed
The European Securities and Markets Authority (ESMA) vs Fitch Group Inc (2019)	Between June 2013 and April 2018, UK-based Fitch Ratings Ltd., Fitch France, and Fitch Ratings España SAU were indirectly owned by an individual who was sitting on the boards of three entities that were being rated by Fitch's subsidiaries. This was deemed to be a significant conflict of interest (ESMA, 2019)	Fitch Ratings was fined nearly €3.2 million, while Fitch France and Fitch Ratings España were fined €812,500 and roughly €1.1 million, respectively
GCR Ratings Vs the Financial Sector Conduct Authority (South Africa) (2019)	The CEO of GCR promised an issuer whose credit rating had expired that GCR would issue a credit rating, contrary to the rules requiring the CEO to act separately from the agency's rating analyst team (FSCA, 2019)	This was deemed a conflict of interest, and the agency was fined R487,000

(continued)

(continued)

The incident/case	A further description	The repercussions and key findings
The European Securities and Markets Authority (ESMA) Vs Danske Bank, Nordea Bank, SEB, Svenska Handelsbanken and Swedbank (2018)	These five banks violated the credit rating regulations by issuing credit ratings without being authorised by ESMA to do so This is a good example of the consequences of issuing credit ratings without being licenced to do so. A similar incident occurred in South Africa, resulting in the entity handing out the rating being fined R 475,000 (ESMA, 2018)	A fine of €495,000 was levied against each of these banks
US Federal and State Authorities vs Moody's (2017)	This was related to risky mortgage securities in the run-up to the 2008 financial crisis (SEC, 2017)	A payout to the US Justice Department, 21 states, and the District of Columbia of $864,000,000—one of the largest fines ever imposed
California's Public Pension System (Calpers) Vs Moody's (2016)	The lawsuit arose from losses suffered by the pension fund after the collapse of the housing market and defaults on securities that were previously rated AAA and backed by pools of residential mortgages (Reuters, 2016)	The courts ruled in favour of CALPERS, and a settlement of $130,000,000 was reached with Moody's in this case

(continued)

(continued)

The incident/case	A further description	The repercussions and key findings
The European Securities and Markets Authority (ESMA) vs Fitch Ratings Limited (2016)	ESMA found that certain senior analysts in Fitch transmitted information about upcoming rating actions on sovereign ratings to certain senior individuals in a parent company of Fitch before it was made public. Furthermore, ESMA found that Fitch failed to have proper internal controls in place to ensure that it provided a rated entity with the minimum time period to consider and respond to a rating action before making it public. Fitch also failed to allow Slovenia 12 hours (the minimum required period at the time) to consider and respond to the downgrade of its sovereign rating in 2012, as required under the CRA Regulation (ESMA, 2016)	Fitch was handed a fine of €1.38 million
King County, Washington et al. v. IKB Deutsche Industriebank AG et al. in the same court, No. 09–08,387 And Abu Dhabi Commercial Bank et al. v. Morgan Stanley & Co et al., U.S. District Court, Southern District of New York, No. 08–07,508 (2013)	Investors accused rating agencies of colluding with banks to award Structured Investment Vehicles (SIVs) with high ratings of "triple-A", even though much of the underlying collateral was low-quality or subprime mortgage debt (Reuters, 2013)	A settlement of $225 million was shared equally amongst the investment banks and the two rating agencies (S&P and Moody's)

(continued)

(continued)

The incident/case	A further description	The repercussions and key findings
ABN AMRO Bank NV v Bathurst Regional Council [2014] FCAFC 65	Standard & Poor's was accused of misleading investors with elevated ratings for financial products, which then lost almost all of their value during the financial crisis (DW, 2012)	The court ruled that rating agencies did have a duty of care to investors, and where that duty is breached, the agency would be liable Damages of nearly AUS$30 million for this case were awarded to 12 local councils in Australia

Index

S. Pillay, *The Next Frontier in SME Ratings*,
https://doi.org/10.1007/978-3-031-54015-8

The manufacturer's authorised representative in the EU is Springer
Nature Customer Service Centre GmbH, Europaplatz 3, 69115 Heidelberg,
Germany. If you have any concerns regarding our products, please
contact ProductSafety@springernature.com

Printed and bound by CPI Group (UK) Ltd, Croydon, CR0 4YY
01/10/2026
02225898-0013